NOEL GALLAGHER

THE BIOGRAPHY

LUCIAN RANDALL

JOHN BLAKE

Published by John Blake Publishing Ltd,
3 Bramber Court, 2 Bramber Road,
London W14 9PB, England

www.johnblakepublishing.co.uk

www.facebook.com/Johnblakepub facebook
twitter.com/johnblakepub twitter

First published in hardback in 2012
This edition published in paperback in 2013

ISBN: 978 1 78219 424 8

British Library Cataloguing-in-Publication Data:

A catalogue record for this book is available from the British Library.

Design by www.envydesign.co.uk

Printed and bound in Great Britain by CPI Group (UK) Ltd

Paper used by John Blake Publishing are natural, recyclable products
made from wood grown in sustainable forests. The manufacturing processes
con[form to the regu]lations of the country of origin.

Every [attempt has been made to contact the relevant copyright] holders,
but some [were unobtainable. We would be grateful if the appropriate] people
[would contact us.]

For Tamsin Mitchell and Miriam Randall

CONTENTS

ACKNOWLEDGEMENTS

I wasn't entirely sure what I would find when I approached a subject like Noel Gallagher. As a star who has been in the public eye for so long he seems to have always been with us. Would there be much more to do than just point at Oasis – look at that? What first interested me was his solo album. It sounded very much as if it had come fully formed from nowhere. A lush, symphonic work, it seemed not only passionate and achingly mature but also to owe very little to Oasis – or at least those early albums which remain what most people know best about them. It was just a guess, but maybe there was another way of approaching the familiar story of this most familiar of bands.

Fortunately, Noel Gallagher turned out to be fascinating

– all I found out about him suggested he was not just charismatic, but surprisingly enigmatic, warm and engagingly contradictory. So thanks are due to him for providing the character to follow here. What I've made of the material I've found is, of course, entirely my responsibility, though to me the Noel Gallagher story was more nuanced than it's been told in the past. In some ways, though probably more seasoned Oasis-watchers might discount this, his life has been one of someone who, despite all his enormous success, has spent many years finding his own voice. For all his confidence and talent that found expression in Oasis, it was *Noel Gallagher's High Birds* that marked him out as having developed into a multi-layered and quietly commanding artist rather than the musical carpet-bomber of the 1990s. This was someone who saw the effects of a hedonistic, rock'n'roll lifestyle and turned away from it. Although not, it has to be said, immediately. This was also someone who left the band he'd spent almost two decades building up and almost immediately began work on not one but two albums simultaneously, one solo and one experimental collaboration. It was an awe-inspiring work ethic he's done well to hide behind the 'fuck it, that'll do' persona the press find so entertaining.

Thanks to John Blake for seeing some merit in the idea of tracing the story from Gallagher's own point of view. Thanks also to Rosie Virgo at Blake, a great friend. Writing this has deprived us of at least one good lunch and that's something to be addressed as soon as this is finished. And I have to say it's always good to work with Blake's Joanna Kennedy too – *dzięki*.

Allie Collins has been a fantastic editor and extremely relaxed about making this book happen on time. She does support United rather than City – but let's just not tell. It goes without saying that any errors and omissions here are my own and I'll endeavour to correct them for any future editions. It's been much harder to get this right than it seemed it would be when I first thought of it.

Stephen Fall provided encouragement and perspective which was extraordinarily helpful and has a seemingly encyclopaedic knowledge of great music. And a very useful library which he kindly shared. Chas Newkey-Burden was also incredibly knowledgeable and provided an inspirational start point for much of this book to flow from. He also carried out additional research and writing without which completing this project would have got very difficult indeed.

Over the years a great deal has been written and said about Oasis. Among the best and most detailed online resources are oasis-recordinginfo.co.uk for the first three albums and oasisinterviews.blogspot.co.uk, a hub of collected interviews from way back. In addition, revisiting 1990s' journalism in the *NME*, *Q*, *Mojo* and the late *Select* gave a sense of the breathless urgency of the times.

The many books providing a perspective on Noel Gallagher include Paul Gallagher's *Brothers* (Virgin, 1996), an account of the early family years by the other brother, co-authored with Terry Christian off *The Word*. The most comprehensive accounts of the era are not just authoritative and exhaustive but also compulsively readable for anyone with even a passing interest in pop. On the scene that defined music in the 1990s, *The Last Party: Brit Pop, Blair and the Demise of English Rock*, John Harris (4th Estate, 2003) and on what happened at its heart in Creation, *My Magpie Eyes are Hungry for the Prize*, David Cavanagh (Virgin, 2000). For a hair-raising insight into the band on the road at their commercial peak, there is the considerably shorter but no less gripping diary account of the Be Here Now tour, *Forever the People*, Paulo Hewitt (Boxtree, 1999). Other useful works included *Going Deaf for a Living*, Steve Lamacq (BBC Books, 2000) and *Was There Then*, Jill Furmanovsky (Ebury, 1997).

Most of all I would like to thank Tamsin Mitchell for her support and cheer as the summer got swallowed up by this project. I wouldn't have been able to complete this without your belief in me and I can hardly find the words to express my love. And also Miriam Randall for being endlessly delightful – by the time you're old enough to read this, people will still be listening to Noel Gallagher's music. And even as late as 1997 who, apart from him, would have been sure about that?

Lucian Randall, November 2012
twitter.com/lucianrandall

CHAPTER 1

HIGH FLYING BIRD

'THE LAST POSTCARD FROM THE OASIS YEARS...'
NOEL GALLAGHER ON 'STOP THE CLOCKS'

Noel Gallagher's High Flying Birds faced an unusual situation when they played on 23 October 2011. Not so much that the gig had come just weeks after Gallagher's debut album had been released and they had to introduce the audience to the new material. But that this was the first time that Noel Gallagher was appearing with his new band since he left Oasis in 2009. This wasn't one of his charity appearances or a guest slot or an acoustic sideline. This was Noel Gallagher fronting his own band.

On one level, of course, there was nothing for him to prove. He was the acknowledged mastermind behind the Oasis masterplan. Over the years he had written not just their hits but the vast bulk of their songs. It had been his vision guiding the band from the moment he had joined them. He had shown he could perform alone many times with the solo sections that had become a regular highlight of Oasis shows. He was relaxed and confident without backup in front of the gigantic crowds the band attracted. When he and brother Liam had one of their almost regular fallouts he might be called upon to take over vocal duties even on the biggest hits. And he had built most of their back catalogue, certainly the ones that everyone remembered, from 'Supersonic' to 'Don't Look Back in Anger' via any number of quieter b-sides. He had taken every song from the very basics of a guitar line to finished album track and he had come to record a number of vocal leads himself on the albums. He hadn't got the nickname The Chief for nothing. Everyone one knew that he was the creative engine of Oasis and there was never any doubt that he could technically do it. But even with the two brothers' relationship was at its tensest in Oasis, there was always the other one around somewhere – even if that was off stage shouting abuse. That October night there was no Liam.

There had always been hints that Noel Gallagher was a front man in waiting. A fully engaged presence in Oasis interviews he took the lead when the two brothers weren't involved in one of their vaudeville banter routines. He was an arch manipulator of the press with an instinctive understanding of what made a great quote. He painted himself as a straightforward lad from Manchester's Burnage, but he could also create as compelling an image of where

Oasis stood in the great lineage of rock'n'roll. More arty bands like Radiohead – who he never lost a comic opportunity to dismiss for being clever but lacking passion in their music – were no more articulate and compelling in their vision.

Yet while his brother might take a secondary role with the journalists around, on stage Liam was more than a foil. His brooding, charismatic presence gave even his tambourine shaking a rattlesnake menace. The unmistakable roar of his vocals, their ebullient sneer and the way he could elongate vowels until they were offensive weapons defined the songs that his brother wrote. And the younger Gallagher kept the band visible even during time off with antics that delighted the tabloids. The very instability of the brothers' relationship had for years seemed to be an intrinsic part of their creativity. It was simultaneously a soap opera and a reminder of real life in a music business that was increasingly engaged in auditioning itself out of real characters with endless talent shows.

Now it was Noel Gallagher fronting the whole show alone with just his High Flying Birds behind him at the Olympia Theatre in Dublin in autumn 2011. The band not only had to carry the weight of expectation felt by any new act but Gallagher had to find some way of presenting himself apart from Oasis. It was an unenviable position for anyone to be in, but Gallagher's response to the questions that hung in the air was characteristically surefooted. He simply embraced his previous life with both arms.

He opened with not a song that was not only Oasis, the aptly-titled '(It's Good) to be Free', but had been the band's first b-side originally sung by Liam on 1994's 'Supersonic'. Gallagher said that it had been included in the set after he had been playing around with the song in rehearsal with his new band and the rest of them all thought it was brilliant. But there was a wider significance to the start of the gig which no diverting anecdote could disguise. This opener was followed by another Oasis track – 'Mucky Fingers' from 2005's *Don't Believe the Truth*. In total the new band played nine songs from the old band – an incredible statement of intent from Gallagher. Here was a man clearly at ease with his old workplace.

When Gallagher's inspiration and friend Paul Weller disbanded first the Jam and then the Style Council, he stayed away from much of their output. Robert Plant was initially shy of including Led Zeppelin material as he established his solo career away from Jimmy Page after the break-up of the band. All perfectly natural. The dissolution of any partnership, from the most intimate to the purely business is touchy and for musicians it can be a mixture of marriage and contractual entanglement. In an effort to define their new personas, ex-band mates will often turn their back on what made them famous, confining familiar numbers to the encore, although with time even the likes of Morrissey has allowed more Smiths tunes to creep into the set. Liam was the same when Beady Eye started in the wake of Oasis as – despite being the old outfit without the Noel – Liam, Gem

Archer, Andy Bell and Chris Sharrock left the old catalogue untouched as they toured *Different Gear, Still Speeding*. But by early 2012, Liam was telling the press that future gigs would include Oasis tracks – 'for anyone who's bothered'.

His older brother simply seemed to feel no need to put the least amount of distance between himself and his previous output, even including such showstoppers as 'Wonderwall' and 'Supersonic' on that very first outing. Questions, anyone? He seemed to be asking. The Chief was getting back to business. Yet at the same time he was far from complacent. As much as he kept control of every aspect of his work, from demo to live sound, Gallagher was also a perfectionist. And as much as he was confident of the quality of his songs, he hadn't been at all sure that the High Flying Birds venture would work until he had a chance to play a few gigs.

'It's easier than I thought it was going to be,' he said. 'I really thought I'd be a grumpy old man about it – I'll just play these songs and if they like them, they like them and if they don't, bugger them – but I kind of feel strangely relaxed about it.' The old band weren't around but he was also now only answerable to himself. If he messed up it was only a problem for him rather than something that affected everyone else in a group partnership.

That Gallagher saw no break with the past had already been established by the High Flying Birds' eponymous album. Second track 'Dream On' dated back to the Oasis years, a slight number written towards the end of the sessions for 2008's *Dig Out Your Soul* and he had even recorded a demo version of it with guitarist Gem Archer. 'If I Had a Gun...' came from the very last gasps of Oasis, having been written around spring of 2009. But these were just ghosts of the old band in comparison with closing track 'Stop the Clocks', which dated back a full ten years or so. A finished version of the track was rumoured to have been in line for inclusion on *Don't Believe the Truth* in 2005 but Gallagher was never happy with the way it turned out. It was dropped a second time from the compilation album which took its name a year later and the fact that he was now finally allowing it to see the light of day was the clearest indication of how he saw his work as one continuous body. The same was true of '(I Wanna Live in a Dream in My) Record Machine'. It was another which had been left off *Dig Out Your Soul*, the final Oasis studio album, and here he re-recorded the instrumentation in a new key to suit his singing voice and added the choir that he had hoped to use on the original version. Noel Gallagher was showing himself to be a man as happy to claim his own heritage as he had done that of other notable bands in rock history when he first started with Oasis.

'I probably won't ever revisit it,' said Gallagher of 'Stop the Clocks'. 'It's kind of like a gift, clearing the decks for what comes next. The last postcard from the Oasis years.' For Gallagher the work in Oasis hadn't run its natural course, even if the band itself had.

And had they not broken up, many of the songs on *Noel*

Gallagher's High Flying Birds would no doubt have ended up appearing in some form on an Oasis release. It hadn't, after all, been inevitable that Oasis would come to an end. The schism between the brothers had been widening for a long time, but then their relationship in public had always been uneasy from the moment they came to prominence. It was this tension that in part drove the band and if anything added to their appeal. Arguments similar to those that any ordinary family might have seemed to help create multi-million selling albums. They would fall out, have a battle of wits and get back together again – sometimes over the course of a single interview. But they always seemed to find some kind of entente cordiale in the end. They were for so long in a state of just about to have a final argument that when it happened for real it seemed more of a shock than had it been a fight that came out of nowhere.

When Gallagher did finally leave Oasis, it was with the end of the Dig Out Your Soul tour in sight. They had been touring the world since August 2008 and there had been disharmony within the band for a while. The end might have seemed to have come out of nowhere as far as anyone outside their immediate circle were concerned – although Gallagher seemed to be increasingly pictured alone or standing slightly away from the rest of the group in documentary footage of the time – but for Gallagher himself much of the tour had been characterised by a background of personal slights. There hadn't been any one particular thing directed to his face but he spoke at the time of how it had got to the point where, if nothing else, Oasis needed to take a break from each other. It was no longer enjoyable. In an interview he gave to Q that June he was talking again about doing something on his own. The last album was already written before they went into the studio but he hadn't even started on the next one. 'I've got a lot of songs lying around,' he said, 'but they're not Oasis songs. They're going to sit there and do nothing, so hopefully at the end of this tour I'm going to go and do something for myself.'

Nothing more permanent had been mooted and still in promotional mode Oasis continued playing into 2009. They returned to the UK from a South American leg where they had found a new generation of fans who had taken the band to their hearts and injected new life into their tour. Back home they began the festival season, kicking off on 4 June at Manchester's Heaton Park for a set of homecoming gigs. These proved not to be in the league of the Maine Road gigs in Manchester of the 1990s. On the first night there were a string of technical problems, starting with a generator failure during the very first song, 'Rock'n'Roll Star'. To grumbles from the fans Oasis were forced off the stage until eventually they declared the gig to be free. 'The curfew's 11, but we'll play until they kick us off,' said Gallagher. 'Keep your ticket and you'll get your money back.' It wasn't clear how this offer would work in practice, particularly as the band recovered their poise and turned in an impressive 23-song set ending, as ever, with 'I am the

Walrus'. Later on in the night Gallagher said, 'Kind of regret offering your money back now. Apply for it back if you wanna be a cunt, we do our best for you.' Those fans who did apply got it via a cheque issued by the 'Bank of Burnage'. There was no shortage of interest in Oasis with three gigs at Heaton Park in total, the third having been added when the dates sold out.

Following festival gigs around Europe, they played Wembley Stadium over three nights – the third also having been added due to demand – from 9–11 July. This hardly signified a band on its last legs and there was still little outward sign of a looming bust-up. Or at least not more of one than usual. While there were exasperated quotes attributed to Gallagher about his brother, it was also said that he had no plans to do anything but go on holiday after the tour finished. Business as usual.

On 22 August they played the Staffordshire portion of the V Festival but the twin gig in the south the following night was cancelled. Noel Gallagher had written on his blog that he wasn't feeling well, but it was his brother's laryngitis which was cited as the reason for the cancellation of what would have been the final UK gig of the tour. They didn't know it at the time but that was the end of Oasis in their home country. They'd gone without a whimper, much less a bang. There were only three more dates left in total, with festivals in France, Germany and Italy and then Gallagher and the rest of the band could take that much needed holiday. They would have finished promoting the seventh

Oasis album around the world and Gallagher could have taken all the time he needed to decide what he wanted to do next.

The first of those last few dates was 28 August and the band were due to headline the first day of the Rock en Seine festival. As it was, they got only as far as the backstage area of the site just west of Paris before an argument broke out between the brothers which ended up in a reported face-off in the dressing room. Gallagher later said he remembered being quite calm, even as he stalked out of the building to seek the quiet of the car which was anyway waiting for him outside. His driver and bodyguard sat up front but nobody spoke. Gallagher considered his next move for a full five minutes, knowing that he was due on stage at exactly that moment. He later said he was well aware that if he told his driver to go that it would be the end of the band. It wouldn't be the first time he had departed Oasis, but this would be different. This would be final. Eventually the silence was broke by the security man asking what they were doing. Gallagher answered, the car pulled away and Oasis finished. As he later recounted the story, he said the Mancunian factor couldn't be dismissed in all of this. This was the way that problems were resolved for lads from the Gallaghers' home town. And there was Noel's perennial enjoyment in making the big gesture. 'There is something pretty special about walking out,' he said with a laugh.

Screens outside relayed the news to fans who initially took the deadpan style to be a joke – 'As a result of an altercation within the band, the Oasis gig has been cancelled.' That other stalwart English group of evergreens, Madness, played their second set of the day in place of Oasis.

The band's website soon carried the news. 'It's with some sadness and great relief to tell you that I quit Oasis tonight,' Gallagher was reported as saying. 'People will write and say what they like, but I simply could not go on working with Liam a day longer.' The news was reported with some uncertainty – even seasoned Gallagher-watchers thought that this could be just another brotherly disagreement. It was left to Noel Gallagher himself to end speculation with a statement that seemed to make it clear that his disagreement with the band went deeper than his youngest sibling. This seemed to be particularly serious.

'The details are not important and of too great a number to list,' wrote Gallagher. 'But I feel you have the right to know the level of verbal and violent intimidation towards me, my family and friends and comrades has become intolerable. The lack of support and understanding from my management and band mates has left me with no other option than to get me cape and seek pastures new ... I would like to thank all the Oasis fans, all over the world. The last 18 years have been truly, truly amazing. A dream come true. I take with me glorious memories. Now if you excuse me, I have a family and football team to indulge. I'll see you somewhere down the road.'

'It's obviously the worst fall-out that they've ever had and they've had some pretty bad ones," said Alan McGee, who had first signed the band to his Creation label. 'But they love each other – they'll come back together ... Whether you're an electrician or a rock'n'roll star, you can only do and be who you want to be. He is the same as everybody else – he didn't want to do it any more and he stopped. People don't do anything now that they don't want to do.'

Gallagher would be candid in the press about the regrets he had in splitting from Oasis, which were perhaps surprising to hear given the deep rift which had opened up. But while there were clearly still many sore points, as Noel talked about his new life he seemed to be very well disposed to his former bandmates. He had socialised with drummer Chris Sharrock and wished all of them the best. In his contact with the press he made it very clear that he was going to draw a line under his previous incarnation and that everyone concerned should feel they could move on. He might not have wanted things to have ended in the way they did, but he was being realistic about it.

'What we did from being a load of working class kids on a council estate with some second-hand guitars was incredible. The fact that we stayed together so long was a miracle,' he said. While he could be roused to temper quickly, he could also remain cool in the most challenging of circumstances. An astute judgement of what worked both in his music and in the business side of things was a key part of what had kept him at the top for so long. Even when Creation was dissolved following the departure of Alan McGee, Gallagher was level-headed in his responses to the press. 'When you go to bed it's a crisis,' he said of McGee's news. 'When you wake up it's just another problem.' He was able to create the same emotional distance as he talked about the band he had led for more than 18 years.

'I think people had stopped listening,' he said of Oasis, adding, 'that's just the way it is when you go for so long. Does anybody care about a new Rolling Stones album these days?' As he saw it, fans of old bands would go and see their heroes play with more enthusiasm than they would check out their new releases. This was a new fact of life in the internet age – artists whose days signed to a record label were long behind them could keep on going with a decent cyber presence and even an album by an act like the Stones was no more than a taster for the inevitable world tour.

Yet Gallagher's blunt summary of Oasis's recent output was reached with the fact of the break-up. While the band was still going he had never thought of them as being in a similar position, despite lukewarm reviews of some of the later Oasis albums. He had then often just shrugged off criticism which had little real effect while the band was still selling its albums in large numbers and he had just kept going. But now Gallagher had the perspective of distance from the old band to reassess what it meant to him.

In 2012 Gallagher talked to the BBC's Mark Lawson for an extended BBC Four interview which touched on the break-up. 'It was never going to end like REM have ended,' he said. Those other elder statesmen of rock had gone from indie status to stadium legends without ever blowing their credibility. They announced an amicable dissolution in September 2011, quickly followed by a final compilation album and promoted by members of the band who confirmed in gentlemanly fashion that they wouldn't play again. Oasis, said Gallagher, 'was always going to end in a fight of some description. Everybody was aware of that. We all wanted it to last forever. I certainly did, but I was always aware that when it came to it that one of us would eventually say, "Fuck you and you and you and you." It just happened to be me. It could well have been Liam.' But even as he spoke he seemed to realise that it would be down to him to end the band, that the element of control had always been with him. He added, 'I think maybe it was inevitable that I would walk out. I've got a pretty long fuse and pretty thick skin until the day that I haven't and then it's just like, "No, no, no... I'm out of here".'

Much had been made of Gallagher's driving ambition and he didn't always seem comfortable with the notion, as if it somehow implied something negative, rather than the creative impetus he felt. 'I've had this reputation since the band broke up of being called a control freak and all that,' he told Mark Lawson. 'And I was,' he continued, glancing directly into the camera. 'And I controlled them all the way to Knebworth and Wembley and all the way to the top of the charts.' And again, Gallagher looked into the camera directly, his level gaze with just a ghost of a smile giving no sign as to whether he was talking to fans or addressing critics or even former band mates. 'So you're welcome.'

Despite his assertion that he had lots of songs ready to go post-Oasis – and it was well known that he was always writing, always topping up his stockpile of killer tunes – he was now out on his own and he was keen to give himself plenty of time to kick back and make plans at leisure. It was left to his brother to make the first move and, always portrayed in the media as the more impetuous of the two, Liam never really took himself out of the public eye. In the aftermath of the split he was interviewed about his clothing line, Pretty Green, and could be relied upon to provide quotes about his brother. More than anything, he never stopped what had been Oasis. Within a couple of months of Noel's departure, Liam announced that the line-up of himself, Gem Archer, Andy Bell and Chris Sharrock would write new material and continue with the addition of bassist Jeff Wootton.

The younger Gallagher had been writing songs for several years and while the number of offerings that made it onto Oasis albums was relatively small, he had quite quickly amassed a large number of half-finished attempts. His brother had been generous in his opinion of those first steps. 'I've got demos of his at home with about 40 tunes,' Noel had said years earlier, 'which, if he could be bothered finishing, would be amazing.' Almost a full decade before he went solo, Noel Gallagher had come close to predicting his brother might end up doing more with his own material. 'He'll be the best songwriter in this country in five years time,' Noel said of Liam in 2002. 'People thought I was being ironic. I wasn't, his new songs are great.' The circumstances were now far from what Noel Gallagher would have wanted all those years earlier, but his praise seemed heartfelt.

With Oasis gone, neither brother needed to continue working – they certainly didn't need to go out separately and try to make their names separately. They might have always seemed to need to prove something to one another, but they both knew that the press and public would be judging whatever they did against the highs of *Definitely Maybe* and *(What's the Story?) Morning Glory*. It was a measure of the passion for music of not just Noel but Liam as well that they were both willing to subject themselves to the ordeal of starting out again. The Gallaghers were jointly worth around £63 million, according to the *Sunday Times* rich list of 2012 and for many aspiring musician the experience of having either written or sung on even one song such as 'Champagne Supernova' or an elegiac moment like 'Half the World Away' would have been enough. Both Gallaghers seemed more driven, but what Noel did next was in a way going to be more of a challenge for him than what he had done first. Because this time around, everyone was watching. There were certain expectations.

It might not have been a battle to compete with the struggles between Blur and Oasis in the mid-1990s, but there was just as much riding on how the two brothers approached their new lives. A bullish Liam was enthusiastic about how his future looked with the new line-up and with the new name, Beady Eye, proceeded without hesitation. Details of recording sessions were announced and their initial single in January 2011 would be the first indicator of what fans made of a post-Oasis world.

In the past, Noel Gallagher had been vocal in how little attention he made to chart placings and he was dismissive of acts which monitored their careers like corporate executives following their stocks. By and large he claimed not to keep up with the fortunes of his brother's outfit. Yet even took notice as news of Beady Eye's reception came in. 'The Roller' peaked at UK No 31 which, as a debut for any other new band, would have been more than satisfactory – coincidentally, it was the position that 'Supersonic' reached back in spring 1994. But everyone connected with Oasis had become used to the conveyor belt of hits and Noel got no pleasure from seeing his brother brought up short. 'I thought it would do what Oasis singles do,' he said when asked by the *NME* if he felt a certain 'glee' at the disappointing figure. '... To be quite honest, it was a bit of a wake-up call for me. 'Cos I was like, right, well, fucking hell, maybe that's what's out there for me.'

The album *Different Gear, Still Speeding* followed at the end of February. It did well, hitting UK No 3 and as an album, well, it wasn't bad. It had the energy and the attitude that you'd expect from Liam Gallagher. The sound was retro-classic, a bit of Led Zeppelin here and a touch of the Beatles there, but subsequent singles failed to make any impact on the charts, while the band toured to respectable responses for the rest of the year in support.

With Beady Eye a fact of life in the music industry, the storm around the bust-up of Oasis eventually subsided. Life moved on, Adele dominated the charts, *X Factor* winners came and went and so when Noel Gallagher made his move, there was genuine interest in him and novelty about his return. It felt like he had properly been away and as a result people wanted to know what he had to say. As ever, he had judged the timing of his entrance with consummate skill.

By the time he did, he had also made a further change to his life – this time in the personal sphere. On 18 June 2011 he married Sara MacDonald – his girlfriend of a decade. He had said that he would never marry again after splitting from Meg Mathews in early 2001, but he and MacDonald already had two sons – Donovan, born 2007, and Sonny, born 2010. 'I just got to the point where I'd introduced Sara as my girlfriend one time too many. I was like, "I sound like Rod Stewart. We should all have the same surname in our house."' Russell Brand was the best man at the wedding. He and Gallagher had a mutual old chum in controversy and when the comedian and Jonathan Ross had got in trouble back in 2008 over rude messages left on the answer machine of actor Andrew Sachs, Gallagher had spoken up for him. 'Yet again, the joyless fuckers who write the columns in the *Daily Mail*, the *Telegraph* or the *Observer* have dictated the tone and are telling people how to behave.' Gallagher had found a kindred rebellious spirit in Russell Brand, both of them operating in their own unique ways in different branches of an otherwise increasingly corporatised media.

Gallagher had been a semi-permanent guest on Brand's show and was a radio natural, going on to sit in for Dermot O'Leary in 2011. During that stint he showed himself to be no more in awe of the BBC than anyone else he'd encountered in his career, mischievously making references to Brand's departure from the corporation following the infamous phone prank. When Gallagher introduced Matt Morgan, who had worked with Ross, to his own show, Morgan self-deprecatingly called himself the sidekick and Gallagher leapt in to tease the BBC, '"Sideshow" Matt on the Russell Brand radio show. Can we mention his [Brand's] name here? Or is his name dirt round these parts? His name is mud, isn't it?' The affection was obvious amid the baiting of BBC suits and it was Brand who presented Oasis with their Outstanding Contribution to Music award at the 2007 Brit Awards.

Like Brand, Noel Gallagher had always seemed to be at home in the media, self-aware, yet confessional and intimate. He was not just adept at giving quotes but putting almost as much into making interviews notable as he did into the music itself. He was a consummate entertainer, with a star's instinctive understanding of timing. He was very skilled at turning awkward questions around and if there was a positive spin he could be relied upon to find it. When critical opinion reassessed 1997's *Be Here Now* as not the triumph it had first seemed, he was the first to agree, but he would quickly add that follow-ups were 'fuckin' mega'. For someone so intimately associated with rock'n'roll mayhem he was a surprisingly upbeat and positive character.

Yet he was also a realist and while he could be deafeningly vocal about his talent and his standing in the rock'n'roll hall of fame, he talked like a man very willing to pay his dues as a solo artist in order to win his audience over again. The month after his wedding, Gallagher held a press conference to confirm the details of his solo album. Ever aware of his duty to entertain, he said he had decided that 'Noel Gallagher' on its own didn't sound 'showbiz' enough. 'It's hardly Ziggy Stardust,' he said. Oasis, for all its plain dealing in its public persona, had been designed to be about escaping the mundane. Not for Gallagher the leap from Style Council to plain old Paul Weller. 'I didn't see my name in lights. I was passing Shepherds Bush Empire [in west London] one night and someone was on there and... I just don't see it.' The line-up was fluid, he said, but if it ever became something more permanent he would just drop the 'Noel Gallagher's' bit. His new trading name itself hinted at a kind of ambiguity in his feelings about the solo life. There was the practical inclusion of his name, so there could be no doubt as to who was behind it – he said the inspiration came from Peter Green's Fleetwood Mac. But then there was the rest of it, as if he was still not entirely sure that he didn't want a band around him.

Of the rest of the High Flying Birds, bassist Russell

Pritchard came from the Zutons, the quirky Liverpool indie band who had come to Gallagher's attention after frequently supporting Oasis in the early 2000s. Hearing that a new band was on the cards, he had simply asked Gallagher if he could be in it. The drummer was Jeremy Stacey, brother of Gallagher's friend and sometime collaborator Paul. Keyboardist Mike Rowe had often appeared with Oasis live and had contributed to *Be Here Now* and *Heathen Chemistry*, while US-born Tim Smith had been in a number of bands such as the quirky American pop act Jellyfish and as part of the back-up for Sheryl Crow. The album's supporting musicians included, from the unremarkable north London district of the same name, the Crouch End Festival Chorus. They were also enlisted by Gallagher to accompany the band on their arena tour in 2012. And the 'High Flying Bird' itself flew in off a track on 1974's *Early Flight*, by US rockers Jefferson Airplane.

The band had impeccable pedigree but the chart experience of Beady Eye showed that success was not at all ordained. Yet Gallagher had been prepared for reality from the start. He had already said he was fairly certain that he wouldn't be doing stadium gigs without Oasis. When a journalist suggested that one man like Paul McCartney could fill a stadium, Gallagher said, 'But then he was in the Beatles... Well – I suppose I was in Oasis!' It was almost as if he needed to remind himself that he could do this thing. He was as blunt about his chances now as he had been confident about the future as a younger man. Almost hesitatingly, he said he could probably fill an arena – at least in Manchester. 'I've not been in this position since *Definitely Maybe*, where it's just like, "We'll put this album out, don't know what's going to happen".'

At the same time as plans for the High Flying Birds were announced, Gallagher said that he was collaborating with eccentric electronic duo Amorphous Androgynous. It was an intriguing counterpoint to the more traditional line-up of his other new band, although perhaps a little too different, as the results seemed unlikely to see the light of day at the time of writing. Amorphous Androgynous had previously provided one of the more sprawling remixes of Oasis's final single, 'Falling Down', clocking in at over 20 minutes. Gallagher had first got in touch with the pair, Garry Cobain and Brian Dougans, after enjoying a psychedelic compilation album they issued. Like Gallagher, the two were veterans, their work dating back to 1980s' act Future Sound of London. It would be far from the first time that Gallagher had dabbled in electronica, having guested before with the likes of the Chemical Brothers.

Gallagher's interest in working with Amorphous Androgynous again showed how wide he was casting his net. It was almost as if he couldn't be sure that rock'n'roll with Noel as a front man would work out and he was going to try all sorts of different projects. Yet while Gallagher confirmed work was advanced with the Amorphous Androgynous collaboration, it almost immediately began to recede into the background. The sessions were reported to be at the experimental end of the studio – and it was easier to see how that was more possible without Liam around. 'He has an irrational fear of keyboards,' Noel had said back in 2008. 'But this is the man who thought we had gone too dance when I wrote "Wonderwall" because the drums didn't go "boom-boom bap, boom-boom-bap".' Noel's attitude was not so straightforward. Oasis would seem to suggest that he adhered to the absolute basics, but he had always been intrigued by the possibilities afforded by embracing samples and loops. His frequent references to Radiohead in interview, although mostly mocking, suggested that something about the process of playing with technology held some kind of fascination for him, however uneasy.

Conventional strings and choir would be a hallmark of the High Flying Birds' album and they were recorded in the same night on hallowed ground for Gallagher, the legendary Beatles home turf of Abbey Road. The guitar sound was also augmented in less traditional ways. When it came to 'The Death of You and Me', Gallagher couldn't make the melody work any other way but on trumpet. He was a long-time admirer of Kasabian, who had come up in Oasis's wake and had indeed been seen as pretenders to the throne. It was their trumpet player, Gary Alesbrook, who he recruited to lead the New Orleans-woozy brass section for the song. It went on to be the first single from the album, with a video shot near Los Angeles, in and around a diner that had been first built for the 1991 Dennis Hopper movie *Eye of the Storm*. Over the chirpy rolls of the guitar, the clip depicts

Gallagher in the diner, writing and gazing out from his table, meeting the prickly gaze of the Mojave Desert through his shades. 'My favourite pastime,' Gallagher said, 'is staring out of the window. When I get on tour I can spend hours and hours just staring out of the window, just thinking of nothing. I love all that.'

The diner provided a setting that was continued in the promos for the next two singles, the follow-up 'AKA… What a Life!' featuring former best man Russell Brand in full flow. More importantly, 'The Death of You and Me', released on 21 August, answered the most immediate question of how the world would take to a Noel without an Oasis by hitting UK No 15. 'AKA… What A Life!' was released on 9 September and that peaked at UK No 20. *Noel Gallagher's High Flying Birds* followed on 17 October and was a UK No 1, also hitting US No 5 in *Billboard*'s 200. The world had decided it liked Noel Gallagher on his own. By 2012, the album had sold more than 600,000 copies in the UK alone, making it a double platinum release, while by contrast *Different Gear, Still Speeding* had managed just over 165,000.

The *NME* was rather equivocal in its review of Gallagher's album in the main, although it did end with a shout of encouragement: 'Fuck radio, fuck the charts and fuck nerves. Noel's still got it. Only a fool would write him off.' Meanwhile, the dependably acerbic Alexis Petridis in the *Guardian* noted of the traditional aspects of Gallagher's writing that some had said that '"Dream On" represents a diversion into "Dixieland jazz": it's got a trombone on it – which in fairness is one trombone more than Oasis ever featured – but then so did "The Floral Dance" by the Brighouse and Rastrick Brass Band.' Even the *Guardian* allowed that for all its conservatism, 'For now, it'll do that it's a more enjoyable album than Oasis' latter-day catalogue.'

And there was certainly no bluster on the album. Gallagher's vocals were nuanced and rather than trying to recreate the swagger of the band he'd left behind, he soaked the songs in the experience of his years. There was an arresting brightness to the album which marked it out as an assured statement. ...*High Flying Birds* never needed to sound like an album with from somebody with something still to prove – but it did. In a way it seemed like the album he had been building up to, sounding all the more coherent and rewarding for not attempting to recreate the primal energy of the first Oasis albums. Its invention and atmosphere were something very different. Gallagher seemed very much to have remained in love with making records. He had said it himself over the years but it never seemed truer than after he left Oasis.

His music was still fuelled by his belief that it should be essentially celebratory. 'Great music is not about real life, it's about how great life can be,' he said. 'Real life's fucking shit!' He was a sentimentalist in his keenness to believe in the magic of rock'n'roll. He might not have been the technological luddite that Oasis had suggested, but he did hate the way the internet bought artists and fans too close. 'Everyone just wants more and more information. All the fantasy's gone out of music, 'cos everything is too fucking real. Every album comes with a DVD with some cunt going, "Yeah, well, we tried the drums over there but..." Give a shit, man! It makes people seem too human, whereas I was bought up on Marc Bolan and David Bowie and it was like, Do they actually come from fucking Mars?'

Meanwhile, Amorphous Androgynous remixes of High Flying Birds' tracks appeared on Gallagher's singles over 2012, including a version of 'Everyone's on the Run' which clocked in at over 15 minutes and dripped with strings and soaring backing vocals. It was disco, dancey and sounded like it was meant to be taken not entirely seriously. This was someone who was having fun and enjoying not needing to make a big guitar statement. But there was no sign of the album that had been discussed between the two and as Gallagher enjoyed his solo success the prospect of it ever arriving seemed increasingly unlikely.

Gallagher explained that the mixes for the album weren't right and he didn't have the time he wanted to dedicate to making it right. But it was also true that the second album was very different to ...*High Flying Birds*. He hadn't said that he'd wanted to see whether rock or electronica would work best, but if he had asked that question, the answer seemed unequivocal. And he simply seemed to be having enough fun getting out with his new outfit. There didn't seem to be any reason to hurry with a new album, though the very fact that he had kicked off solo life by working on two albums simultaneously was interesting in itself. At the height of Oasis mania in the 1990s, he'd often been depicted in the press as a party animal who had simply got lucky with a revivalist rock band. But his work rate now, in his 40s, belied that caricature. Underneath the Oasis rock'n'roll stereotype seemed to lurk a driven and imaginative creative force.

The High Flying Birds tour became markedly bigger into 2012. They would go on to play summer dates into September, including festivals and arenas, which made Noel Gallagher one of the biggest solo artists in the UK. He had adapted to what could have been a daunting change. 'Oasis was a big cruise liner and now I'm like a Sunseeker speedboat,' he said.

At T In The Park in Scotland on 7 July, the soap opera headlines which might once have tracked Oasis were all about the reunion of the Stone Roses but the High Flying Birds preceded them with a set that nevertheless commanded total attention. As a live proposition, Gallagher always had a look about him that spoke less of the rock star aura than it did of an expression of concentration on his playing that might be mistaken for mild exasperation. Yet the audience notably sang along to all the new songs as much as the classics from the old band. He concluded with 'Don't Look Back in Anger' and, as had become customary, left the choruses to the fans. They were still singing them after the band had left, a whole field of people holding the band's presence for just a few more minutes, many of them too young even to have seen the last line-up of Oasis perform the song live.

The doubts and the critics were silenced in 2012. The Scottish performance came midway through a tremendous year which had begun in great style with a Brit nomination for his new album and the *NME* Godlike Genius award – the recognition of lifetime achievement which had previously gone to Primal Scream and Gallagher's own friends and influences Ian Brown and Paul Weller. Things had panned out to a perfect balance for Gallagher, succeeding on his own terms and yet playing gigs of a size manageable enough for him to give b-sides an airing which would have been lost in the stadium years of Oasis. But Gallagher had always been good at remembering what it was like to want to hear the less obvious numbers in a band's catalogue as a fan himself – 'I used to go and see the Smiths and they'd always play those fucking brilliant b-sides and I'd always think, Fucking hell, "This Charming Man" is great but "Rubber Ring"? That's the shit!'

On stage for the first time with his new band at the Olympia in Dublin in late 2011, Noel Gallagher had emphatically realised the potential inherent in ...*High Flying Birds*. He'd craftily become an accomplished front man over 18 years almost without anyone noticing, but then from his earliest years he had always been good at learning as long as it hadn't involved going to school. From the days when he first realised how much music moved him, he had soaked up influences and carefully watched how the industry worked.

It had seemed unlikely that Oasis would ever survive past their first or second album, but Gallagher's upbringing and first steps into the Manchester music scene made him uniquely placed to take the industry and make it his own.

CHAPTER 2

BURNAGE, MANCHESTER

'A BLOODY GOOD FRIEND TO ME IN THE '70S...I WONDER
WHERE HE IS? I THINK HE ENDED UP IN REHAB.'
NOEL GALLAGHER ON HIS CHILDHOOD ACTION MAN

Noel Thomas David Gallagher was born on 29 May 1967.
His parents Thomas and Peggy Gallagher were from
Ireland and he spent the first few years of his life in
Longsight, Manchester. Noel's father worked in the
building trade, a labourer, and was a DJ in Irish clubs as a
sideline. The family had three sons. Only 16 months
separated Noel from his older brother, Paul Anthony, who
was just seven months old when Peggy got pregnant for the
second time. After the birth of the youngest, William John
Paul – Liam – in 1972, the family moved further out in
Manchester, settling in a bigger house in an estate in the
suburb of Burnage. It was better than Longsight, but an

unremarkable area and marked a childhood that Gallagher never felt the need to spend much time revisiting.

'I remember the '70s constantly being winter in Manchester,' he said, 'and the Irish community ... closing ranks because of the IRA bombings in Birmingham and Manchester, and the bin workers' strike, all wrapped up in it... They were violent times. Violence at home and violence at football matches.' It wasn't an easy upbringing for any of the Gallagher boys in the household.

The dependable centre was Peggy Gallagher, every inch the warm-hearted, family-orientated Irish mother. She was born in County Mayo in Ireland on 30 January 1943 and was the fourth of the 11 Sweeney children with seven sisters. Having moved to Manchester, she was married to Tommy on 27 March 1965. Today she still lives in the city, in the same council house that her sons were brought up in. Their family and friends are also in the area and even her estranged husband remains nearby in the house they occupied until the night she took the family away. He has always been around, a visible presence on the streets, though they haven't spoken for years.

Much would be written by others about the harshness of Gallagher's upbringing – both he and Paul would develop stammers – but he was himself keen to stress in interview that he wasn't as affected by it as had been suggested. If it did mean more to him, it didn't seem like had been brought up to be the type to share it in public. His early years shaped him, he said, but he would point out that the times themselves were tough. His father, said Gallagher, was not the monster of legend, but he was 'a shit dad'. He was prone to outbreaks of violence and Gallagher, who thought that young Liam inherited the short fuse, said that he was on the receiving end of it. But he would also later say that he preferred not to think about the past and not to revisit what had gone on a long time before. He didn't want to be defined in his later life by the place he'd come from.

On one occasion when Tommy was ill the family had some time away from him. 'He was taken into hospital for an operation on his spine and it was nearly two months before he came home,' said older brother Paul. 'They sent him off somewhere to convalesce. For a couple of months we had a sneak preview of what life would be like without him around.'

In 1984, Peggy finally moved the family out of their unstable home life in the middle of the night. 'There was nothing in it,' Peggy wrote of their new home, 'only the four walls and the sink in the kitchen. The council offered me the house on the Monday and I told them we could move in on the Friday night when their father had gone out. Tommy went out that Friday night as usual and I knew we'd be gone when he got back. I arranged for my brother-in-law, George, to come over to help us. We were still moving stuff out at 2am – it was a real midnight flyer.' Noel remembered being relieved that his father wasn't around, thinking of the 'bedlam' as he later put it, which would have ensued.

Peggy Gallagher was left to bring up the three boys and, despite other family and friends, she was essentially alone with lads who could be a handful – not so much Paul, but certainly Liam and Noel too. 'She did it,' said Noel. 'She gave it all up for us.' It was in some ways a rerun of Peggy's own childhood, in that her own father – in turn not a warm man with his family – left home when she was around seven

Noel never made any attempt to see his own father after Peggy moved them that night, despite always knowing exactly where he was. It was left to the *News of the World* to engineer a meeting between the brothers and their father at an Oasis party more than a decade later, but despite what must have been a tremendously fraught occasion Noel was careful to keep as calm as he could about it. Later he would say that the encounter made little more impact on him than ruining what was a great night out and when all the fuss died down he reverted to his policy of no contact. Forget the past. As he pointed out himself, plenty of people had been having it just as bad when he was growing up. That was, after all, the late 1970s and the early 1980s.

Gallagher was 12 when Margaret Thatcher became Prime Minister in May 1979. If you said to Burnage residents then that the young Gallagher would be invited to meet the next Labour Prime Minister in Downing Street in the mid-1990s, among the many reasons why nobody would believe you would be how unlikely it seemed that the already unpopular Conservatives would cling to power for the next 18 years. But those would be dark times for huge swathes of the population, particularly those in the declining manufacturing strongholds of the north. Work was scarce and Gallagher himself spoke of how ordinary and drab everything seemed to a kid in the area.

'We were all on the dole. My dad was on the dole at some points. My friends were on the dole, as were their dads. It was a pretty bleak time.' Yet he would never write about his childhood through his lyrics – at least not directly. But the very fact that he blanked it so completely in favour of the rousing sentiments of vague positivity which characterised Oasis was an indicator of how far he wanted to move away from that place and time. He would always remember the experience of having to go the job centre to collect dole money with his father. And, although he didn't think too much about it, he had imagined that most of the other children on his street would have had similar home lives.

Gallagher pointed out was also one for playing up, soon taking to going out half the night and getting up to no good. 'I was a tricky customer,' he said. 'I was a bit lippy, you know.' He was often described as moody. It wasn't a description he recognised in himself, but he allowed that he frowned a lot. Smiling just wasn't in his nature, he said, but almost as an aside he would add that he didn't feel he had a nice smile.

Growing up, Gallagher was just like most of the kids in the area. Like his brother he was of average height and was a very normal, unremarkable lad. 'When it was time for Noel to go to school,' his mother later wrote, 'he was very different from Paul. He loved it and mixed in well with the other kids. Once Noel started going, it helped Paul to settle down and get more used to it.' All that changed as Noel got older when it came to secondary school – which it generally didn't if he could help it.

He joined a large, Catholic and was immediately put in the top classes due to an administrative error. As he recalled, there was an unrelated Gallagher in the same intake who was destined for academic heights and they had inadvertently swapped places. It wasn't until the first school holiday that it was realised that by mistake the other Gallagher had been 'left with all the oiks. I don't think he's ever recovered! He probably had a nervous breakdown or something.' Noel was swiftly put in with the other crowd: 'So when I got down there... Ah! These are my kind of people, down here! This mob, sat at the back.' He had almost immediately decided that school was not for him. Looking back at his time there, it seemed to be not so much that he was unhappy or had difficulties as such – he just didn't see the point. Once he could read and write there was little there to detain him apart from creative activities such as art and sport.

It was very easy simply not to go to school and there was a sizeable group along with Gallagher who made the choice. They would hang out together, sometimes going to a house where they knew the parents would be out working. Even then, Gallagher was 'obsessed', he said, with music – so were most of his friends – and they would all listen to records whenever they could. The Beatles were first – there was always the Beatles. He might have been far too young to have seen them, but they were always on his radar.

Top of the Pops was another huge influence – and not just for the music. It was the whole institution of the show that began in 1964 and was a fixture of television for decades. Peggy Gallagher would be charmingly bemused by the way her son went from avid viewer to performer. 'She's going, "Oh, I used to watch you watching Bono on *Top of the Pops*",' Gallagher later said. 'And now she can say, "I was watching you, watching Bono, watching you, watching the camera, watching me, watching you." It's like – "Don't ever get into smoking pot, Mam."' Such was the affection for the show throughout the country that it was kept on life-support long after it had ceased to matter. But until the late 1990s its countdown of the nation's favourite tunes mattered in a fundamental way. It would be *Top of the Pops'* rivalry between Oasis and Blur which would provide its last real moment of power in the mid-1990s. Gallagher was entranced by its reporting of the glam glory years, with the androgynous likes of Bolan and Bowie enlivening the evening. Later he was more conscious of the Sex Pistols, though still a bit young. His early years were spent in the company of bands like the Who – he would not only later count them among his friends but would also play live with them. But it was the Jam which was the first band he thought of as being his and he recalled seeing them perform on *Top of the Pops*' more serious brother, *The Old Grey Whistle Test*.

Music provided a much-needed escape from reality. Peggy would later recall that Noel had been a daydreamer even as a child. He was otherwise the classic middle child, self-contained and capable and not given to overt displays of emotion – a true Northerner in that way, he would speak of how he didn't shed a tear as he walked away from Oasis in 2009. But the daydreaming and the practical side soon came together in an early talent for compelling storytelling. 'Whether we were playing cops and robbers or cowboys and Indians, Noel would never die gracefully,' said Paul Gallagher. 'He'd say you missed.'

And even when he was going AWOL from school, he was careful to leave home with satchel in place and return with a detailed account of what had gone on that day. Then Peggy got a phone call from the school to say that he hadn't turned up for three weeks. 'I had other things going on,' said Gallagher of his pre-teen self. 'I was busy.' His mother was furious when she found out, if anything more by the deception than by the actual truancy. His scheme was complicated by the fact that Peggy was a dinner lady at the same school and Gallagher had to become adept at being able to eat lunch without spending any further time in the building. He worked out how to evade the teachers and would make sure his mother saw him before making good his escape. If nothing else, he was at least well-nourished by his time at school.

For Gallagher the truancy was just fun – it wasn't his way of making a larger point and he had plenty of friends who were the same way. He did feel he was more disliked than most by the teaching staff at the school. There was nothing more to it than that disapproval, but it seemed to him at that young age as if he was continuously in his headmaster's office, offering his hand up to be strapped. He felt that anything that ever went wrong in the school was in some way made to be connected to him, somewhere down the line. 'I'm not saying I was wrongly accused of anything,' he later said. 'It was usually connected to me somewhere down the line...' But this wasn't a case of his obvious intelligence and ability going unregarded by the school – he had simply never turned up enough to give himself a chance to prove otherwise.

For children in his area at that time, education was just not necessary because there was nothing around them to indicate that it might be worth harbouring ambition. That was the way he remembered it. Nobody managed to make him believe that by being educated he might be able to better himself in some way or find fulfilment. He didn't connect with the notion of school in any way. Everyone he knew ended up in the building trade so all the trimmings of a comprehensive education was utterly pointless. It was just a question of measuring out the time before Gallagher reached his destiny in life – labouring.

The only alternative that anyone ever thought of – and most boys his age had harboured the dream – was football. Not all the traits that Paul recognised in his brothers from their father were positive, but this was one he did trace back with fondness. 'One thing we gladly inherited from him, though, is our support for Manchester City Football Club. League champions in 1968, FA Cup winners in 1969, League Cup in 1970 and League winners in 1976.' It wouldn't be until 2012 that City won another league title. They were 'the team for the boys: the young scallies. Noel and I, together with our mates, agreed that we'd all have plenty of stories to tell our grandchildren about our jaunts across the country to see our heroes in sky blue.' United fans, by contrast, were a different breed. They would go to matches with their families rather than their friends and they would have to book tickets up well in advance. United fans even had season tickets.

Noel would become almost as famous for being a lifelong Manchester City fan as he was for his time in Oasis. Football came into his life before anything else – music, *Top of the Pops*, girls, all of it. At the very height of their fame, Gallagher was asked by a journalist if Oasis were more important to their young fans than God. The mischievous reference was unmistakeably to John Lennon and his 1965 comment that the Beatles were more popular than Jesus – 'I don't know which will go first, rock'n'roll or

Christianity.' The line was unremarkable at home but led to orchestrated album burnings in the God-fearing USA. Gallagher got the joke but gave it a serious spin. 'Now that's a loaded question!' he said. 'Football is more important to me than religion. Some of the pop stars I like are more important to me than God, so yeah.' Football... music... God. He'd gone one better than his hero Lennon and put religion in third place.

When Gallagher did get to God, it was largely out of duty. For years Peggy Gallagher would go to church and Noel would also be a regular Sunday attendee. Eventually – with some relief – the family stopped. But when he started to be serious about song writing, religion would be an intriguingly common theme. For him though, as much as he revealed in interviews, there was no great meaning in his references. It was simply that he wrote anthems and there was nothing more appropriate to back the dramatic chords and searing melodies of Oasis hits than talk of God and all the rest of the instantly recognisable paraphernalia of the church. Safe to assume from what he said that it was all just useful window dressing.

And yet, when Oasis played Mexico City in March 1998, Gallagher took what he described as a pilgrimage to the ancient city of Teotihuacan, abandoned in mysterious circumstances even before the Aztecs came on the scene, much less Spanish conquistadors. It was an area rich with myth and legend. For some archaeologists the collapse of the region was a pre-environmentalist warning, its citizens having used up too many resources and come under too much pressure. For Gallagher, the possibility that some kind of alien intelligence was behind the two dramatic pyramids which dominate the site was at least as intriguing. It was said that Gallagher had read up on the site long before he visited it and it was one of those occasional hints that however little he talked about belief he had least retained ambivalence about it in general.

He gave the question of God some space, though he was quick to point out that, 'I don't think that anyone in their right mind would believe it's a guy with a beard in a one-piece tunic, living on a cloud, playing a harp.' Yet for all that, he also said at the same time that, 'God is a fascinating concept'. For him it was just that it was a more straight-forward idea. 'Seemingly,' he said, 'everyone has their own perception of what it is. I don't know what my perception of it is. I don't know whether God is within you and it's just your own version of it in your soul or what.' But he was wrong to assume that everyone had that view – for those who really don't believe at all, God simply doesn't register. You have to have an open mind to the idea to think of a God at all. Gallagher might have simply been talking as someone with an active imagination, constantly looking for arresting pictures to create in song. But his words didn't bear that out – he didn't sound like the committed atheist it might be expected a hedonistic rock'n'roller to be, even if he was never what anyone would call a true believer.

Football, on the other hand, didn't come with any

question marks and Gallagher showed some ability. 'Noel was quite skilful, a silky little player and fairly nippy on the ball,' said Paul. 'But he'd shy away from a bruising tackle so he never fulfilled his potential on the football field,' Noel himself didn't feel he had much talent, but it didn't matter to his love of it or how he felt it represented a way out of ordinary life. Being a footballer was something he could picture, in a way he could never quite imagine being a pop star – there were far fewer in Manchester who made it in music that than became footballers. Pop stars never came from Burnage. They were 'bussed in' as he later memorably put it, from somewhere else. Somewhere not here. In a more general sense in Manchester, there was always Joy Division and New Order and the Smiths to look up to, but they were esoteric, unreachable. Until the Stone Roses came along there didn't seem to be a believable role model. Nobody in his area even went to gigs much.

Gallagher didn't look to his younger brother to follow him as he began to become interested in music. While Noel was getting into his teens, Liam was still very much a kid. The two shared a bedroom but Noel had five years on him and for children that kind of gap had real significance and they had little to do with one another. Noel would later say that the brothers never really got on, telling one interviewer in 1995 that the youngest Gallagher didn't even have the decency not to 'be a bird. At least then I could have gone out with his mates.' But he was speaking when the band was at its height and they were jockeying for their position in

43

the world, in Oasis and as brothers. Their volatility was always played up in the media. There was another side to it. Gallagher would also talk about how Liam would turn to him on the rare occasions that he was nervous about performing and it was clear that the older brother looked out for him. Liam was the more impetuous, taking to the role of front man with enthusiasm, something which Noel would come to with greater reluctance. It was Liam who would end up the more regular inhabitant of the tabloid gossip pages, reliably keeping the Oasis name in the public eye when they were resting between albums and the increasingly grand world tours. Noel wanted the world to know how good they were and for everyone else to get a chance to hear his songs while his brother always seemed to need approval from everyone – Noel included. 'Whenever he plays you a tune he's written,' Gallagher later said of his younger brother's forays into writing, 'he expects you to be in total awe.'

After Oasis, with their position in the world secure, Gallagher was more measured in his assessment of the brothers' relationship over the years, even saying that they got on well enough as kids. The closest he got to a problem with his sibling, he said, was that Liam was constantly borrowing a fiver from him. It was only when success came with its ferocious speed and overwhelming size that their relationship began to shift. But one element remained unchanging throughout the good and bad years for both brothers and that was the encouragement of their mother.

She was not judgemental and was incredibly loyal towards all three of her boys. She wanted them to feel fulfilled in whatever they did.

As well as her school job, Peggy had worked in a biscuit factory with perks that led to a nickname for Noel with classmates. 'Come home from school,' he later said, 'and you'd have two ham sandwiches, a tiny little bottle of milk and about 60 Penguins and 70 Jaffa Cakes.' On the rare occasions he attended school, he remembered, her job 'made you dead popular at school ... "Here comes Gallagher 'the biscuit'."'

Yet it wasn't easy for Peggy to manage financially while bringing up the three boys herself and that was something that pickings from the biscuit factory couldn't hide. Noel tried to, though. Paul remembered, 'Noel would spin stories to the kids saying we had this and that and we'd done this or that. I got a bit resentful about his stories ... because he had a way of making stories interesting and funny. It niggled me.'

But in a way, Noel was only developing his ability to be positive about whatever came his way and that was something that Peggy had encouraged. He said that their mother instilled the knowledge that if he wanted things to happen he would have to do it for himself. Nobody was going to give him anything in life. He had to get on with the routine of each day himself. The boys all took this on board. Theirs was a very pragmatic family unit, not given to big displays of affection, but close. Peggy had one of the boys' cousins from Ireland, Willie, stay with them for a while. Later on, as the band took off, Noel put Willie on the guest list for a gig at the Sheffield Arena. But Noel and Liam themselves would become more like band mates than brothers, rarely seeing each other outside of Oasis in later years. They were never been the sort of family to exchange Christmas cards once they grew up. And when the split did eventually come, they would simply stop talking.

The phenomenon of brothers in bands has always had mixed fortunes. Most famously, Ray and Dave Davies of the Kinks, a favourite band of Gallagher's, argued for so long that they even produced songs about their relationship – among them 'Hatred (A Duet)'. Into their 60s they would still be duking it out though to some extent, as with the Gallaghers, the urge to do better than the other brother had perhaps sharpened the Kinks' creative powers. At the other end of the scale were bands like Sparks – essentially brothers Ron and Russell Mael. Despite the title of 1970s' classic 'This Town Ain't Big Enough for the Both of Us' they seemed to get along amicably over their long career in a disappointing fashion for any easy theory about sibling rivalry.

Noel Gallagher himself would hear enough of the various hypotheses about the pathology of brothers in arms to become exasperated when an interviewer mentioned the Black Crowes. Chris and Rich Robinson had also fallen out countless times over a career that ran almost in parallel with Oasis. And their bluesy output had a similar sense of traditional rock about it. 'Oh fuck that,' said Gallagher when a comparison was made with him and Liam. 'We handle it pretty well ... I've only seriously tried to kill him once. I think that's a pretty good record.' In a wry nod to the battles often documented very much in public, Oasis joined with the Black Crowes and Spacehog (their brothers were Royston and Antony Langdon) for series of US dates in 2001 called – what else? – the Tour of Brotherly Love.

With Gallagher's facility for a good yarn, his own familial arguments played out over the years in the press would take on a cartoonish quality and he invariably arrived at interviews armed with one with a good punchline. He memorably conjured the image of his brother getting to grips with mobile phones when they first became popular and how he used his to send late-night messages of ill will to Noel, albeit sometimes not entirely lucid ones. 'And he'll claim he has no recollection of any of it,' said Gallagher. But the subtext was always the same: '"You're a cunt."'

Noel and Liam had a different relationship again with their older sibling Paul. Not quite as certain about his path in life, he was never in the limelight and that put him at a remove from the intensity of their professional trajectory. Yet there were certain public expectations that came with being a Gallagher brother and the effect on him was to reverse his connection with Noel, who he felt 'was in many ways like an older brother. He probably wasn't as daft and impressionable as me. I think a lot of younger brothers have a certain amount of thinly disguised scorn for their slightly older siblings.' When he was asked to think back to their childhood in his own book, he remembered Noel as likeable, friendly but quiet, an observation which was relayed to Noel himself in interview. He responded with an enigmatic chuckle. Paul also recalled that one of his brother's favourite toys was an Action Man he took everywhere with him almost as some kind of security blanket. 'He was very military-minded,' said Paul, 'between the ages of three and seven with loads of toy soldiers and tanks.' Noel himself would always remember the best thing about his Action Man – it had moveable eyes.

The three brothers got out of Burnage for the summer holidays most years, spending weeks back in the Irish countryside which had been home to their mother's family. Their uncle, Paddy, who lived in Yorkshire, would drive them across to the ferry at Holyhead and from the other side to the peace of County Mayo. For Paul the important point was they were able to 'escape from our dad'. Noel, like the other two, seemed to like it well enough but it didn't make that much of an impression. Being around family was a little dull and perhaps he was just too much of an urban kid to find much to inspire him in the nature of Ireland.

Gallagher just about made it through his school career, such as it was, and had somehow found himself still there on the last day, when he became involved in an incident in which a teacher was flour bombed. Guilty by association even if he didn't actually do it – 'I was definitely there, laughing my bollocks off' – Gallagher was expelled at the very end of his time in education, something which he thought was particularly petty on the part of the school authorities. He didn't even receive a leaving certificate.

There was now the question of what Gallagher should do with the rest of his life. He was 15 now and doors were never likely to be flung open. He was rooted in his home town with its limited options. In the past he had flirted with petty crime, but, he said, he had known that if he got caught he was going to get some kind of punishment. 'I'm just glad I didn't go to borstal,' he said. 'I wasn't a great criminal. I was nicked pretty early and I was, like, It's not for me, I haven't got the criminal gene.' Everything pointed towards becoming a labourer. He would end up the buildings, just as it had always seemed he would when he was at school. Anything more creative was just never an option. Not only had no major cultural icon come from Burnage, but he felt that here the very idea of performing was viewed with suspicion. The way he later talked about trying to get into music in Burnage it seemed as if in general the arts were regarded as somehow not masculine in themselves. 'I'd risk certain death if I was seen by any football hooligan,' he said. It would have been a case of: 'Who do you think you are with a fucking guitar, you fucking poof?'

Having maintained a semblance of contact with his father despite his parents' break-up he worked for some time with Tommy Gallagher's own concreting business, as did Paul.

Both brothers had also helped out with their father's DJing, carrying boxes of records and equipment to the clubs. Even that limited engagement soon ended. Peggy later wrote, 'After they stopped working for him, he never once tried to get in touch with them, never wrote to them and never supported Liam.' Noel was left to pick up other jobs wherever he could. Sometimes there was nothing. When he or either of his brothers were out of work, his mother was conscientious in ensuring none of her boys simply laid around the house all day.

'You do what you have to do,' Noel later said, 'because your mam boots you out of bed at 11 o'clock in the morning and says, "Get down the fucking job centre!"' But at the same time she was – as long as they were doing something worthwhile – always supportive. Even when her middle son spent concentrated periods of time playing guitar.

Gallagher said he was 13 when he picked up the guitar which stood behind a door in one of the rooms in the home they then still shared with his father. It was only Noel who showed interest in playing it and he was never quite sure why it stayed around the place. 'Unless,' he mused years later, 'me mam's a secret bluegrass picker...'

Paul remembered there had been both a guitar and an accordion hanging in the same place which had belonged to their father, who would 'dabble' with them. As did Paul himself. 'I was the first to get a guitar and Noel used to play with it,' he wrote. In his recollection Noel had been interested in the guitar even longer than was later reported.

'He'd have been about eight then, which is six years younger than Eric Clapton when he started playing. Our Noel was really into the guitar and could play it better than me, despite the fact that I jealously tried to restrict his time on it and refused to show him any more than a few chords. In the end our mam bought Noel a guitar out of the catalogue for about £25-30 and paid it off weekly. He was seriously into playing the guitar, like some junior junkie. He'd have taken it to the toilet with him if he could – he probably did.'

Gallagher was left-handed, but would end up playing that first guitar with his right rather than re-stringing it. Taking time given to him when he was grounded over 1980 – which was a frequent occurrence – Gallagher began by working out the throbbing, melodic basslines of Joy Division's Peter Hook. Noel would work them out on one string at first. Once he had worked his way through other classics like 'House of the Rising Sun', the next step that same year was to experiment with writing his own songs. It was, he later said, what everyone does. But this wasn't true. Many people never get further than strumming the basics. His older brother was one example. For some reason, songwriting was just in Noel, though vaguely at first and it wasn't something he would really develop until he joined Liam's band. But whatever it was that kept him going, he persevered with the instrument.

'Noel strumming on his guitar was an incessant but almost comfortably familiar sound in our house at night,' said Paul. 'Then he got an electric guitar and an amp it was, "Hello, rock'n'roll will never die." He'd crank the volume up and have that guitar squealing out all kinds of tunes and riffs.'

Towards the end of 1980 Gallagher got his first taste of live music. He couldn't have made a better choice for a blast of musical high drama and sheer demented fury in seeing punk pioneers the Damned at Manchester Apollo. They tore through classics like 'Neat Neat Neat' and 'New Rose' and Gallagher was blown away. 'I couldn't believe how loud it was and how tall the stage was,' he told a musician's magazine years later. 'I'd only seen concerts on TV, where the camera is level with the band. When I saw the stage all the way up there, I was really struck.' That same year, he also lost his virginity – it had been a busy first few teenage months.

The room that Gallagher shared with his younger brother was increasingly filled with evidence of his developing love of music, with records, stereo and guitar. By the time he was 16 his influences had widened to include local boys the Smiths. It was the look as much as anything – guitarist Johnny Marr had that classic rock outfit – black clothes, shades and the shaggy haircut. But despite the fundamental love of all things guitar-based, Gallagher could hardly spend his formative years in Manchester and not encounter club culture. Even the most traditional of musicians were having their heads turned by the loved-up ecstasy scene that had transformed Gallagher's passions. Football was changing too as a result of the drug. The hardest supporter 'firms' in the country had got into the drug as it spread throughout the country in the late 1980s and into the 1990s. The terraces were awash with loved-up hoolies and the beery violence of earlier years fell away, for a while at least. Part of the domestication of football was also down to the vast amounts of money that would come with the Premier League and later still the all-seating rules that followed the Hillsborough Stadium tragedy. But ecstasy had also played its part in influencing football and formed a link with the music scene in clubs.

The times were fertile for the developing acid house movement, though as a musician you didn't have to be into drugs or electronic music to appreciate good, danceable tunes in a club. There were absolute classics in old R'n'B that Gallagher later told journalist Paulo Hewitt, an intimate of his circle as Oasis became successful, he was never asked about because it was assumed he wouldn't have any interest in dance, soul or rap. 'Pisses him right off,' wrote Hewitt. 'No one asks, "What do you reckon? Jackson Five or Sly Stone." The answer, had anyone asked, was 'Sly Stone. Of course.'

The point was that, in truth, Gallagher's influences were wider than his later public persona as a rock absolutist would suggest. 'We used to say this thing when we were in the Haçienda, off our heads,' he said in 2012, 'standing in front of these big speakers listening to acid house music for the first time, going, "D'ya wanna get *inside* the music…"' He was a devoted clubber between 1987 and the formation of

Oasis – though there were, as he said later, limits: 'Never raised me hands in the air once, though. When we went to raves, they used to go, "Let's see some hands!" and I'd go, "You're not fucking seeing mine, pal".' But the feeling he got from it – the emotion rather than the message of lyrics that came with guitar bands – never left him.

Years later, armed with a copy of iTunes, he managed to track down the classics which thrilled him back when dance music was primitive, transgressive and new. He would later claim he could date when dance music stopped being a dark art mastered only by a cabal of pasty-faced musical scientists and just another branch of pop. In the process he revealed he knew as much about dance music as he was famed for knowing about guitar bands. He had the same level of passion for all sorts of music and he hated it when any musical movement lost its power. 'Any fucker can do it. And, quite frankly, every fucker is doing it,' he said. 'Back in the late '80s to get those songs like "Pacific State" [808 State] and "Voodoo Ray" [A Guy Called Gerald] and "Strings of Life" [Derrick May], they're just amazing. Amazing pieces of music. And no words! And that's what used to bend my head. It's like every kind of popular cultural thing has somebody, whether it be Johnny Rotten or Mick Jagger preaching some form of manifesto.' And he admired the way that, while the spark came from the US, it was fuelled and transformed in the UK. For Gallagher it was the most original form of music for decades. 'It happened because it had to happen. Rock, or rock'n'roll or indie guitar music, whatever you want to call it, had fucking come to a dead end.'

Hip hop label Def Jam staged a UK package tour in 1987 with acts including Run DMC and LL Cool J. The intention was to put on a show that demanded attention. Air raid sirens opened Public Enemy's set and Chuck D later said, 'You had the so-called British invasion of America by the Beatles 20 years before and we thought of this as the reverse, a hip hop invasion.' Gallagher was watching when the forces reached the Manchester Apollo and later said that the 1980s had been a time 'when rap was inspirational. Public Enemy were awesome.' NWA's incendiary and controversial debut *Straight Outta Compton* came out in 1998 and if nothing else he would later nod to its influence with a sample on *Be Here Now*.

Gallagher's own experience of producing music had its earliest expression through local bands he messed around with. He and a friend named Paul Bardsley played as Fantasy Chicken and the Amateurs. They would each take turns to write songs and sing. By 1986 and into 1987 Gallagher was beginning to record his own demo tapes on a four-track portable home studio, this time with Mark Coyle, who later worked on *Definitely Maybe*. The results were surprisingly polished and fast-paced with titles including 'I am the Man' and 'I Didn't Think So', songs that betrayed a Morrissey-flavoured vocal style.

An initially less welcome influence on his development came as a result of an accident. When he broke his foot on site at work he was confined to non-physical work and he used that period to improve his playing and writing. It was then that he worked on what would be 'Columbia' and 'Live Forever'. 'Up until the night I wrote "Live Forever",' Gallagher recalled, 'I was writing a certain kind of music ... I always go back to that song as being the pivotal movement in my song writing.'

To get a flavour of the Manchester music scene that Gallagher was wanting to find his way into you would have to look no further than its current bands. In 2012 it seemed that every major act from the time was – however unlikely it might have seemed almost quarter of a century ago – back on the road. The summer of 2012 would be dominated largely by the blockbuster Stone Roses reunion but elsewhere Happy Mondays were also and most improbably of all, back together. It wasn't just the northern sound – there was more from what had been Brit Pop as Blur played a blockbuster gig in London, though Damon Albarn was even then hinting that he couldn't see himself working much longer with his old gang. Pulp and Suede were also back together in some recognisable version of original line-ups. But the nostalgia seemed particularly active in Manchester. While more brand new bands than ever competed for playing space in the city all attention was on the past. Even Inspiral Carpets were on the comeback trail – but not, it was safe to assume, with their original road crew intact. At least, one guitar tech in particular would be unlikely to be reporting for duty.

Just after his 21st birthday in May 1988, Gallagher celebrated by going to see James play at the International II in Manchester. It was a home town gig for the band organised by the Northwest Campaign for Lesbian & Gay Equality in opposition to the Conservative initiative to ban what they alleged was the 'promotion' of homosexuality in schools – widely known as Clause 28, from the local government act in which the legislation appeared. It was a very worthy event. But for most people there, the big attraction was support act the Stone Roses, another key influence on Gallagher. Not one given to lavishly praising other bands without reason, he told one journalist years later, 'For me, personally, I wouldn't be sat here talking to you if it wasn't for them.' It was that simple and the Roses were at a pivotal point, a year before their eponymous debut would begin to change the way that indie music was perceived in the mainstream. More immediately for Gallagher they were a band who were individuals recognisably like him. A hint that he could do it as a boy from Burnage. And in time, lead singer Ian Brown would become a friend and collaborator.

It was that night that Gallagher got talking to someone he noticed recording the gig on a cassette recorder. This was one of those chance encounters which, if not quite Mick Jagger's 1961 meeting Keith Richards at Deptford station, was to be the start of a musical career for Gallagher. Not only did Graham Lambert offer to do a copy of the gig but he revealed that he was guitarist for

Manchester's Inspiral Carpets, who were at last enjoying a mainstream hit as their anthemic 'This is How it Feels' had taken its soaring chorus to UK No 14. Gallagher was soon friends with Lambert and the band even asked him to audition when singer Stephen Holt left towards the end of 1988 to form the Rainkings. There was, however, one problem.

'Couldn't sing a fucking note,' Gallagher later said. It would be years before his singing style was something he felt confident with. He could demo his own songs and he would take over singing duties when required, but for a long while singer was not a role that he initially felt comfortably in filling. That wouldn't come until Oasis were famous around the world. The Inspirals' consolation prize was the position of roadie and he immediately accepted, leaving his latest labouring job in early 1989.

This was also the year after he had decided it was about time he should be leaving home to move in with girlfriend Louise Jones. 'He was always the steady type,' said brother Paul. Noel had already had an engagement as an 18-year-old with a previous girlfriend named Diane from nearby Levenshulme. As serious about his new girlfriend, Gallagher remembered his mother being mortified when he announced his departure and trying to argue him out of it, almost as if he was much younger than 21. She loved all her boys and just wanted them to be around her, but Gallagher needed the freedom of being with Louise on a full-time basis and they moved into her flat together. She was, said

Paul, 'his first big love ... Louise [was] really into going out and clubbing and she's quite tough with a strong personality. Noel needed and liked that about her.' Through his new job he was also beginning to see there might be a way to get to the world not just outside home but outside the UK itself.

The Inspirals were just becoming successful after years as an indie band and their city was beginning to get into the scene that would soon be known throughout the country as 'Madchester', that euphoric, hedonistic yell of musical confidence from somewhere that wasn't for once the south. Happy Mondays, the Stones Roses, the Charlatans and countless acid house acts were all riding the wave that soon came to indiscriminately include virtually anyone who came from the city. Now rock was sucked into the dance and football mix to create the knowing, laconic brand of pop that came to define the next couple of years and would create the space into which Oasis would later step. It couldn't have been a better time to find out what life on the road in rock'n'roll was all about.

Gallagher got to travel not only through Europe, but as far afield as the US, Japan and even the newly-opened frontiers in the east in Russia. He wasn't simply lugging equipment around – sometimes he would do press when the band weren't around, he'd set up what they needed when they went partying and he also got to figure out how the stage gear worked. He was also becoming a good all-round musician. If not a front man by nature, he was shaping up to be someone who could have been the classic session player. He was up for depping for the Inspirals' drummer when he became sick at one point and could turn his hand to keyboard when required. As part of the crew he would be sound checking on stage and would take the opportunity to play his own songs. Standing on stage himself, having his own band suddenly seemed possible. 'I could easily do this,' he remembered thinking. 'I just need to find the right people.'

He was incredibly enthusiastic about the world he had found himself in and Inspirals singer Tom Hingley later said that Gallagher, just as he had once done in his bedroom at home, would play guitar 'all day'. By the time the band themselves got up for their soundcheck they'd sometimes even find the batteries in their guitar effects pedals were dead. Through the band he was at last getting on with like-minded people, including sound tech Mark Coyle, who helped him out with his four-track demos.

The Inspirals were in Munich as part of a European tour when, in the course of Gallagher's weekly phone call home, he was stunned to hear from his mother that Liam was 'rehearsing'. The age gap suddenly caught up with him as he thought back to the years when his younger brother had taken no notice of the music in their bedroom, the guitar or Noel's playing of it. Now he was hearing that his brother was not only in a band but he was the singer.

On his return he went along to see the group play. Here

was another jolt. 'They had something,' Gallagher said. 'I was shocked at him on stage.' The shock was that Liam didn't look out of place.

CHAPTER 3

AFTER THE RAIN

'THEY ALL DIE AT 27! I WAS ONLY JUST
KIND OF LIMBERING UP THEN.'
NOEL GALLAGHER ON ROCK STARS

In August 1991, Noel Gallagher went to see Oasis play. The local band fronted by Liam had been formed as The Rain and it was Liam who had changed the name. The inspiration was in itself a microcosm of what would make the band successful – blending the legends and mysterious creativity of rock music with the determinedly down to earth. For while Oasis might conjure images of mirages in spice-tinged heat, Liam had in fact taken the name from the Oasis Leisure Centre in the M4 corridor town of Swindon. Which was a desert of sorts.

Liam had been recruited in April 1991 to the band of 21-year-old guitarist Paul 'Bonehead' Arthurs, 20-year-old drummer Tony McCarroll and 20-year-old bassist Paul

'Guigsy' McGuigan. All Manchester lads, except Lancashire's Guigsy. Liam had taken their new name from one of Noel's Inspiral Carpets tour posters. Noel himself was already aware of the other three from a local park where a big gang of them used to gather to muck around and pick the local magic mushrooms. More usefully for the new venture, Gallagher had amassed invaluable knowledge about the music business in his life on the road, but he made it clear he wasn't interested in filling the available role of manager. He was looking for a creative outlet for all the ideas that he'd been working out over the years on his guitar.

His arrival was later characterised as that of a Mancunian Svengali, whose presence in the band was paid for by the other members ceding control to the man who would be Chief. His brother sometimes referred to him as Noely G, a fluffy nickname that served only to underline his true dread purpose in that context. Noel Gallagher himself would waver between living up to the legend when it worked well in the early days and later distancing himself from it, pointing out that he hadn't arrived on the scene fully formed. But even if the masterplan wasn't quite in place at that point, none of the band would deny that his songs were good and he was soon on guitar. It helped from a practical point of view that he had just been given a payoff from Inspiral Carpets and had been earning a decent salary with the band. It meant that he came to the new band with some resources behind him.

Yet the idea of Noel Gallagher as the all-powerful, the

dictator, would be an attractive one to propagate as the band established itself, whatever the truth. Gallagher himself would later suggest the first gig they played consisted mainly of songs that the band were already playing before he joined. But though it would be him who was long responsible for all the songs that appeared once the band was signed, that also meant he was under much more pressure as the albums kept coming. He might have the control and the publishing royalties but it meant that all the creativity fell to him and that could become a source of frustration with time. To begin with though, the song writing bug bit and it bit hard. 'When I heard my songs being played back to me by this band in a room,' he said, 'something happened. And then I started to write furiously.'

More than anything his ferocious output was such that it was almost by default that he became the song writer. 'I never said to anybody else, "You are not allowed to write songs. This is my thing".' Perhaps the others might have welcomed the chance to contribute something if things had been different, but in those early days it also suited everyone in the band to have a strong character to the music. Gallagher's songs had a very clear definition. The classic chord progression, the slow chug of the verses to their singalong choruses, the non-specificism of the aspirational lyrics, the simple but soaring melodies. These elements were what made Oasis so special for so many and that was the speciality of Noel Gallagher. Years down the line he would assert that it would have been helpful for other band members to come up with songs much earlier in the band's life, but his imprint was overwhelming. His wasn't necessarily the most advanced musicology in the world in those early days, but it had a personality you could see a mile off. When other musicians did contribute songs – albeit much later – it was marked how much they sounded Noel-esque. He had a definite idea of what he wanted his writing to achieve and that was more of the feeling he had experienced through his interest in club music rather than the meaning he got from the music of other guitar bands. 'Even if it's about nothing, I know what kind of nothing it's about,' said Gallagher.

Having never set out to change the world with words, he was up for anything that made the job easier. When a journalist, somewhat horrified, later picked up his mention of using a rhyming dictionary, he laughed at how un-rock'n'roll it clearly made him sound. 'Afraid so, afraid so... I never wanted to be a lyricist. So I have to use everything in my power, really and I'm afraid rhyming dictionaries are one of the things that I do use when I get stuck.' Writing seemed to be very much only another tool to get him where he wanted to be.

Yet he didn't believe the band was just about him or his brother, as much as they had swiftly moved to the front. There would be many personnel changes down the years, but he never changed his view that there was something very specific about every aspect of Oasis, even down to the unadorned drumming. 'If you start overplaying it, it kinda doesn't fly,' he later said. 'You can't be Keith Moon. Particularly on the older stuff 'cos it was never about the drums.'

He also had a deceptive work ethic. As Oasis set about rehearsing, despite the reputation they developed for living the rock'n'roll lifestyle to the limit, under Gallagher they were dedicated to polishing the bombastic style that would become their trademark. At the same time, it was all very much in the spirit of punk. Nothing complicated. None of the band could read or write music, but then they hardly knew anyone who could back then. Gallagher later said how he had never got much further than major and minor chords and the mysteries of modes, diminished chords and the like never concerned him. His rehearsal ethos went straight back to the basics – pick up the guitar, put some chords together and then tell the rest of the band, 'It goes like this.' Early songs such as 'Columbia' were designed to make it easy for the band to get into. 'It's just a groove – everyone plays the same chords all the way through, then our kid sings, then that's about it,' he said

The new Oasis played their first gig on 14 January 1992 at the Manchester Boardwalk – the same venue they used to rehearse. They didn't have much money and their prospects didn't immediately look bright but the mechanics of playing were very easy at that time. Gallagher was living with Louise on Whitworth Street in the centre of Manchester, just a few minutes stroll away from the venue. He was already talking the band up at their first outing. Even at this stage, there was a confidence and attitude in Gallagher that was reflected in no way at all by the reality of their situation. 'There was 40 people maximum there,' he told Q magazine, 'and we had a song called "Rock'n'Roll Star" ... People were going, "Yeah, course you are, mate, bottom of the bill at the Boardwalk"...'

But it wasn't just attitude in the face of indifference. Gallagher was formidably determined to make something of his band and his own songs. A demo tape including live tracks was sent around to no great reaction and Gallagher personally went to see Tony Wilson, Factory Records' legendary boss, broadcaster and a Manchester personality of a size to match that of either Gallagher. But that too came to nothing. Gallagher's response was to continue writing, rehearsing and playing. Oasis got to showcase at the inaugural In The City in 1992, Tony Wilson's incubator for new music set up in Manchester. The band played alongside other unsigned acts Radiohead and Suede. It was turning into a hard slog getting noticed, though by November they were attracting audiences of around a hundred to Boardwalk shows.

Gallagher continued to tell anyone who listened that Oasis were going to be massive and was greeted by deafening disinterest. He was now reaching 25 and in pop years that was approaching obsolescence. Madchester had long lost its edge, gone national and given way to the dance groove of baggy, this being less defined as a scene aside from its adherents determination to look hip. Baggy didn't exactly have the visceral importance of something like punk. 'I think a lot of people in Manchester just gave up after the Madchester thing,' Gallagher said, 'and sat on their arses and didn't do anything.'

Gallagher's experience with the Inspiral Carpets didn't seem to be paying off. It was probably just as well that he hadn't confined himself to managerial duties with Oasis. But then came the break – another one of those lucky meetings – that would allow him to hand control to someone who really knew what they were doing. Having run into the brother of Johnny Marr on a night out at the Haçienda, he handed over yet another one of the Oasis demo tapes. Since the Smiths split in 1987, Marr had joined the Pretenders before forming Electronic with Bernard Sumner from New Order and providing guitar for indie polemicists The The. Marr was sufficiently impressed with what he heard to put the tape forward to his own manager, Marcus Russell, whose Ignition management company also had Bernard Sumner and Neil and Tim Finn – Crowded House – on their books. This was more like it. By May 1993 Russell would be Oasis's manager.

Gallagher knew there was more to be done on the band's sound. Better quality demos were recorded of 'Columbia', along with 'Bring it on Down' and 'Rock'n'Roll Star' – all of which would make it to the debut album. Meanwhile, Gallagher had talked another band into letting him use their eight-track studio and the difference showed. And it was another local band who gave a second, more decisive, shove in the right direction. Oasis shared their rehearsal space at the Boardwalk with the all-girl Sister Lover. Their Debbie Turner knew Alan McGee of Creation Records and had a gig supporting one of his recent signings, 18 Wheeler. The gig was all the way up in Glasgow and she suggested that Oasis come up with them.

On 31 May, Oasis made the 200 mile journey from Manchester to north of the border. They were making for a tiny venue called King Tut's Wah Wah Hut and were essentially going on a whim. The gig wasn't their friends' to give and they arrived to find the bill was full, three other bands already booked. The night gave birth to another legend about the band – and, like the one about Gallagher having arrived fully-formed in Oasis, it was also to be enthusiastically relayed by everyone in those early years. This version of events had the band stalking into the promoter's office, shutting his door on the outside world and telling him that if he didn't let them do the gig then King Tut's would that very night burn to the ground. But as Gallagher himself pointed out later, 'Anybody who's been to Glasgow will know you don't get away with that kind of shit up there,' but it would be a useful myth to have around as the band got going.

Oasis's future label boss knew all about the importance of a good rock back story. Alan McGee, like Tony Wilson, was a music business veteran with a big personality who had the Jesus and Mary Chain among many others as proof of what could be achieved through reputation. Mary Chain gigs had been characterised by roiling waves of disorientating feedback and chaotic performances which energised audiences, caused riots and did no end of good to build their name. So when it came to Oasis it didn't really matter that the real tone of the band's request to get on the bill was rather more pleading and that they were readily given 20 minutes to play as the doors were opened – it was no big deal to the promoter – as the story made them sound impressive before anyone had heard of them.

What was never in doubt about that night in Glasgow – and in a sense was more amazing than the hard nuts stories that were dutifully spread through the press – was that they did manage to play this minor gig as the doors opened and Alan McGee just so happened to have turned up early. 'I'd had by this point about four or five double Jack Daniels and coke, so I was, like a bit wavery,' McGee later said. When the first of Gallagher's song sounded brilliant, he put it down to his mood. Same with the second. But when the third came, he said, 'I thought, I'm gonna do it.'

A band like Oasis might well have made it anyway and Noel Gallagher was clearly never going to give up, but this was nevertheless the kind of one-in-million example of serendipity which would be rejected from a movie about a wannabe band for being too much of a rock'n'roll dream cliché. But McGee wandered up to the band at their table afterwards and asked Gallagher what they were called. Then, did they have a record deal? No. Did they want one? Yes. McGee said, 'And he [Noel] gave me a demo tape and I went, "You're all right, you don't need to give me a tape," and he went, "No, take the tape," and that was that.' An enthusiastic McGee woke up record label staff in the middle of the night to tell them so. 'I've found them!' he said. He was convinced that this was the band to make Creation's fortune. But his staff had heard it all before. Yet everyone at the label was as passionate about music as their boss and even though he'd been excited about bands who'd gone nowhere, they were all up for going for it again. When they heard the tape, though, particularly 'Live Forever', the rest of Creation began to see why McGee was so fired up in the middle of the night.

The next morning both Oasis and McGee decided they still respected one another. The band made a trip to London to meet Creation and Oasis were soon on board – though Paul Gallagher later noted that they didn't sign until October, when their manager was in place and Noel, ever watchful, was certain about everything. But Gallagher was at last on his way – he hadn't joined a band until he was 24 and now he had his first record deal at 27. 'They all die at 27!' he said. 'I was only just kind of limbering up then.'

And indeed the 27 Club – that rather harsh term for those like Jimi Hendrix and Jim Morrison who left the party early – was just over a year away from gaining another prominent member. Nirvana's front man Kurt Cobain was struggling to follow up their massive hit *Nevermind* with something meaningful. *In Utero* would be the rather uncertain result that September, while grunge continued to dominate the charts in all its plaid-wearing, doom-mongering, US-based glory. The genre would be something that Gallagher could virtually define himself against. Oasis would be everything that grunge and Nirvana weren't – not least in the seeming misery that worldwide success brought Cobain.

Much closer in some respects to the developing Oasis and to Gallagher was Jarvis Cocker. He was almost 30 and was still battling for recognition in Pulp. Their musical styles might have been worlds apart, yet both Cocker and Noel Gallagher were defined by their regional identity, their vision of what their music could achieve and a stubbornness in making it work for them on their own terms.

More immediately, the effect of the deal was to boost Gallagher's productivity and he began to churn out so many songs he would be holding some back for years to come. Many new artists end up worrying that they've used up their best numbers on their debut, but some of his would become live favourites and gain legendary status by the time they were recorded. A case in point was 'All Around the World', which Gallagher would be bigging up for years until it was eventually recorded for 1997's *Be Here Now*. He insisted that it was the best song he had ever written, though by the time it came out it faced strong competition from other quarters of his output.

Exposure was coming slowly for Oasis. In August they were played on BBC Radio 5, with 'Cigarettes and Alcohol' on Mark Radcliffe and Marc Riley's show, while they also continued gigging around the country. One of their early tours was with the Verve – the Richard Ashcroft-led outfit who they would support, be friends with and outstrip – and another band whose outlook was very similar to Gallagher's. Gallagher would later dedicate 'Cast No Shadow' from *(What's the Story?) Morning Glory* to Ashcroft, who would in return dedicate 'A Northern Soul' from the 1995 album of the same name to him.

By the end of the year the crowds at gigs hadn't grown significantly, but there was already a sense of something about to happen. On stage Oasis were Bill Wyman-esque in their reluctance to move unnecessarily, not so much encouraging the crowd as challenging them. And yet there was an energy about them. Keeping the momentum going, Gallagher and the rest of the band moved directly from the live push to the studio.

'Supersonic' could have referred to the speed that Gallagher worked in those early days. What would be the first single was recorded in one day – and that included the writing time. When things came together for him, Gallagher was a sprinter. The idea had been to do a version of 'Bring it On Down' but the band kicked off with a jam which sounded too good to leave. Gallagher sat in a corner out of everyone's way and wrote the lyrics in around ten minutes. The Beatles made their influence known with a nod to 'Yellow Submarine' and, along with references to notions of betterment and an overarching sense of defiance, the song set the pattern for much of Gallagher's writing.

The identity of 'Elsa' in the lyrics would remain a mystery and a focus of all sorts of wild theories until

Gallagher revealed it was a Rottweiler with particularly dubious hygiene hanging around the studio. Even when the origins were revealed, Gallagher maintained, any number of girls called Elsa tried to claim they were the inspiration. He got the letters from the would-be musical muses. Meanwhile, he added ruefully, his brother would be pursued by 'all these sex-starved young girls with big breasts'. But the origins of the song, much less the sense of the lyrics, were never the point. It was the overwhelming guitar, the soaring soloing that grabbed at its listeners. There was no attention paid to nuance in Gallagher's early work. Once a song was written, there was no discussion of what it signified. 'It wasn't that kind of band,' Gallagher later said with a laugh.

Liam would get on with the business of delivering the lyrics but the brothers didn't talk interpretation. Noel had a definite sense of how he wanted the lyrics to sound, how the melody went and it was here that he said he and his brother would argue. 'But we'd get to a place where it was acceptable,' Gallagher said. There was not necessarily a reason for the sound that either of them was aiming for, or at least not one that either of them would articulate. It seemed to be very much a case of them squaring up to one another to set out how they instinctively felt the words should be sung.

The single was held back while the band went on to record *Definitely Maybe* at the start of 1994, when it seemed that the ease of their first day in the studio had been beginners' luck. In the end, the album would be recorded twice before they were happy with it. The first go around with producer Mark Coyle, who had known Gallagher since they were both roadies with the Inspiral Carpets, didn't give the band the big, guitar-drenched sound they wanted but, more worryingly, the second attempt wasn't nearer. This time they had the opposite problem, with far too much guitar. Gallagher was too close to it and was increasingly frustrated with the failure to capture the magic that made the band so vital. It was then that Owen Morris – who also went into the studio with Oasis soul mates the Verve – was brought in to work on the album and was such a good fit that he stayed with Oasis until they began recording *Standing on the Shoulder of Giants* in 1999. His first job was to strip away a lot of surplus tracks to get to the essence of the work and reveal the essential energy that lay underneath.

The result showed how Gallagher had an enviable facility for song writing. Only 'Digsy's Dinner' seemed superfluous and perhaps 'Sad Song' could have substituted for it. Even 'Married with Children', while slight, was a better vehicle for the Gallagher sense of humour. While he always worked hard to amass a catalogue of songs, he also said that the melody and the music came easily to him. 'That's in me,' he told Mark Lawson in 2012, 'I don't know where that comes from.' He would play around with a set of chords for months, fascinated by their progression and if it was the beginnings of a song that he found he could stick with, at some point a melody would arrive – it was really that spooky and primal. It was harder for him to find the words to hang around the melody line and a process that he found could be frustrating, at least until he learned just to wait and see what came.

While the recording process was underway, the band hit the headlines en route to a gig in Holland in February. They had taken a ferry to Amsterdam, when Liam and Guigsy were detained amid trouble at the onboard bar and had to travel back separately to an annoyed Noel without playing. But the media loved it. The band were building a real buzz and yet were already creating headlines before they'd even released an official single (though a promo version of 'Columbia' was issued at the end of 1993). The Dutch story was redolent of every badly-behaved Brit onboard and abroad, the hooligan holiday-makers or football fans beloved of *Daily Mail* leader writers. Here was a band for middle England to be outraged about and for music fans there were overtones of the Sex Pistols celebrating the Queen's 1977 jubilee with their cheeky Thames boat party. As reports came of the Gallagher brothers arguing over the affair it seemed, thrillingly, as if anything could happen. They might even split up before they'd properly released more than a single.

Yet Gallagher was determined not to lose it, though there would be more shenanigans and each story would be followed eagerly by the press. On 9 August they played the Riverside in Newcastle. Not at their peak performance, the show only got worse when a fan clambered onto the stage and Gallagher was injured in the resulting confusion. As the band left and the gig descended into chaos the *Daily Mail* headlined its carefully nuanced report AN ORGY OF VIOLENCE. But away from the background roar, Gallagher was convinced *Definitely Maybe* would be the most important release of its era and pointed at tracks such as 'Rock'n'Roll Star' to define the mood. It was everything that Gallagher wanted from his life. As a writer he was able to think back to being a kid and receiving revelations from first encountering the Beatles and the Stones. 'I hope that when people put this album on in years to come,' he said on its release, 'there'll be some kid bouncing around a bedroom with a tennis racket to "Rock'n'Roll Star".'

But as much as it was a statement of intent, *Definitely Maybe* was also simply about having good friends to have a good time with. There were those light-hearted numbers – 'Digsy's Dinner' was inspired by a friend who did indeed ask Gallagher over for tea and promised Italian cuisine. 'Married with Children' was along similar lines, but then there was 'Slide Away', a moment of introspection. It was a rare example of a love song which Gallagher had written with girlfriend Louise Jones in mind. Yet the couple, who had been living together since he left home back in 1988, split just two months before the album came out but the song was a favourite for fans – and it was Gallagher's personal high point, at least at the time the album was first released. 'It's just about being in love,' said Gallagher. 'Not for very long, unfortunately, but that was how I was feeling at the time. I wanted to write a song that was somewhere between "Cortez the Killer" [Neil Young] and "Wild Horses" [Rolling Stones].'

The band's first TV appearance was on the show with a reputation to match the one they were themselves fast making. *The Word* was cheeky, badly behaved and frequently told off, the very model of a Friday night Channel 4 youth TV programme. Host Terry Christian remembered that the London-centric makers had to be convinced to have a fairly unknown Manchester band on at all. His girlfriend and Louise Jones both worked for Red Alert, the company responsible for getting exposure for Oasis among other edgy new acts such as Inspiral Carpets and Björk.

The 18 March edition of the show was to be the last of the series and 'on the night itself they sounded fantastic,' wrote Christian later, with the show's main guest, Bob Geldof, saying how good he thought the band were.' It was a programme known for its partying and the last night bash was no exception. But Oasis acquitted themselves with the charisma and wit of bands much more established, remembered Terry Christian. 'Noel was on form, taking the mickey out of England fans, saying that most England supporters supported crap teams like Huddersfield Town.'

They played alongside the likes of Soul Asylum and hip hop act the Kaliphz. Paul Gallagher said that Peggy was glued to the show. 'On that particular Friday night she had two of her beloved sons playing in their own band in front of a TV audience of 2.5 million people,' he wrote. 'She cried her eyes out, she just couldn't help it. She felt so proud.'

CHAPTER 4

UP IN THE SKY

'DEFINITELY MAYBE WILL ALWAYS BE SEEN AS ONE OF THE GREATEST EVER DEBUT RECORDS, BUT I ALWAYS KNEW WE COULD BE EVEN BETTER.'
NOEL GALLAGHER

Gallagher was convincing in his belief that Oasis was going to go all the way. 'Everybody else said the words, but I actually believed it,' he said later. He was single-minded about making the most of the potential in his band. He had seen other bands who could have gone all the way fall out, lose it with drink and drugs or succumb to the pressures of life in the music business and he was determined that Oasis weren't going to blow it. By April 1994 Nirvana's Kurt Cobain had just done exactly that.

It was in the Lake Washington district of Seattle on 5 April, as 'Supersonic' was about to hit the charts, that Cobain killed himself. He'd checked himself out of detox and after a few days lying low, he at last successfully committed suicide with a shotgun, having long seemed likely to do something along those lines. Grunge would continue to exert a hold on the press through the likes of Pearl Jam and less directly the Smashing Pumpkins and had if nothing else, shown what happened when you combined the DIY ethos of punk with metal. An indie sound could become world famous. Grunge had also meant the music press focus had been on America. There just wasn't anything of comparable size happening back home. Now, just as happened back in the 1960s, the Brits were about to reinvent rock and sell it back to the world.

'Supersonic' was released in April with a video in which Liam got to show off the monkey walk patented by the Roses' Ian Brown while the band performed outside as planes zoomed supersonically overhead. Was 'Supersonic' playing intentionally dumb? It didn't really matter as the record-buying public would get the broad play from the start. Knowing that they were at last going to receive some airplay, Gallagher and the rest of the band went to Paul Arthur's house and huddled around to listen to themselves on BBC Radio 1 FM. At the appointed time, the steady beat started and the scraped strings rang out. 'They said our band's name, the band that we'd been in for three years that was going fucking nowhere,' recalled Gallagher. 'I sat there, like, Wow, well, this is it. Where the fuck is my private airplane?' It wasn't quite on the tarmac yet – 'Supersonic' peaked at UK No 31 and the follow-up, 'Shakermaker' illustrated the dangers of Gallagher's penchant for going through musical back pages. There was enough of a similarity in a portion of the song for the New Seekers to mount a successful legal action over their early 1970s evergreen, 'I'd Like to Teach the World to Sing (In Perfect Harmony)'. It wouldn't be the last time that Gallagher got in a copyright pickle.

In what was a busy spring for music, April also saw the release of *Parklife*. Blur were onto their third album, but now they reached national consciousness, with 'Girls and Boys' having preceded the album to reach UK No 5 and become ubiquitous among students and holiday discos alike. The clever ambiguity of the lyrics and chirpy keyboards provided a frothy attitude at odds with the straightforward creed of Gallagher, although both bands had a remarkably similar way with the catchiest of tunes. But at this point you didn't have to define yourself by whether you were team Blur or team Oasis.

Trouble continued to dog the northern contingent, as they toured in the year while mania around the band escalated with each single in the run up to the release of the album. And Oasis themselves did their bit, serving up their own generous portion of mayhem on the road as 1994 wore on. In a quieter moment in June they played as part of the Creation Undrugged night at the Albert Hall in London. When Liam had a sore throat, Noel decided to play the few songs they had to do himself. It was his first real opportunity to front up the band himself and he acquitted himself well.

As with Undrugged, so it would be with MTV's *Unplugged* a couple of years later – and as on the later occasion, Liam turned up to observe his brother's performance from close quarters. But the singer was back as they played the NME Stage on Sunday at the Glastonbury festival and continued to impress alongside the likes of Blur, Radiohead and Spiritualized. Backstage, Gallagher met Paul Weller and was delighted when he said he liked 'Supersonic'.

Much of the public excitement about Oasis was down to the band's attitude. They weren't serious like the grunge bands, they weren't tricksy like Blur. The third Oasis single, 'Live Forever', accompanied the release of *Definitely Maybe* in August. 'I don't believe in that ethic of live fast and die young – which is what the song "Live Forever" is about,' said Gallagher. 'I hope to live to be 390. But what will be, will be. I believe everything is mapped out for you anyway. Nothing gets me down about life in general, nothing pisses me off.' The song had been one of those Gallagher came up with while recuperating from his work accident. It had been a staple for the band performing live and the sleeve now featured a picture of John Lennon's childhood home in Liverpool. This was designed to have an appeal for anyone.

As work was finally completed on the album, it was discovered that it was too long to fit on a single vinyl record, so to make it up to a double, Gallagher added 'Sad Song', providing an interesting counterpoint to the generally upbeat mood of the CD version. Along with the big moment that was 'Live Forever', *Definitely Maybe* was a

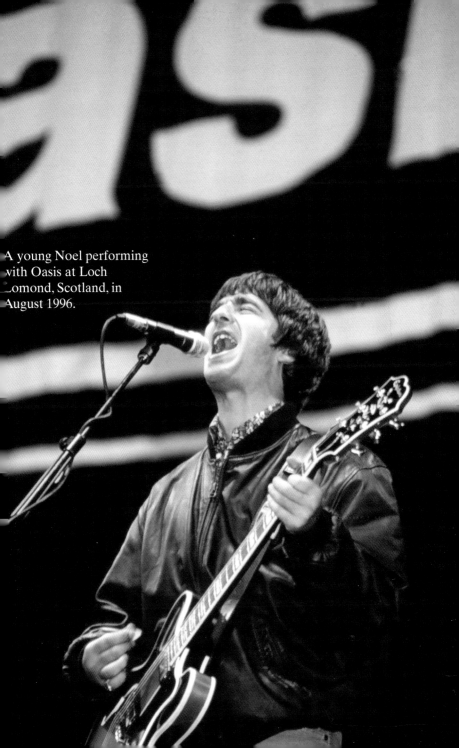

A young Noel performing with Oasis at Loch Lomond, Scotland, in August 1996.

Top: Noel singing at Earls Court in London, 1995

Bottom: Noel and his brother, fellow Oasis member, Liam, accepting an award at the 1996 Brit Awards where they won Best British Group, Best British Video and Mastercard British Album.

Top left: Noel and his then wife, Meg Mathews, at a party hosted by Tony Blair
at 10 Downing Street, 1997.

Top right: Oasis concert at Earls Court, London 1996

Bottom: Shaking hands with Tony Blair in Downing Street, 1997. Oasis were at the
centre of so-called 'Cool Britannia'.

Top: Meeting Tommy Hilfiger (*left*) and Goldie (*centre*) at a Tommy Hilfiger Party in London, 1999.

Bottom: Noel with his brother, Liam, in September 1997.

Top: Noel, Meg and friends Kate Moss and Lisa Walker at Sound Republic, London. 1998

Bottom left: Noel and Meg Mathews at the film premiere of the *Blair Witch Project*.

Bottom right: Noel in concert with Oasis in Frankfurt, Germany.

Noel and his mother, Peggy, sharing a joke at the *Irish Post* awards.

Top left: Noel posing with Oasis' *NME* award for Best Music DVD, 2005.

Top right: A touching moment between Noel and his girlfriend, Sara MacDonald, at the Reading Festival in 2001.

Bottom: Noel having presented an award to Stephen Merchant (*left*) and Ricky Gervais (*centre*) at the British Comedy Awards 2004.

Noel performing at the Fair Play
concert for Oxfam at the London
Astoria in 2002.

hedonistic celebration of youth, Gallagher telling an enthusiastic audience that there was no need for deeper meaning when you could have such fun. 'You feel like you're 18, you've got a great new jacket on and you're going out to kiss the fucking sky,' he later said. This was the soundtrack for the *Loaded* generation, the 'new' lads. It didn't matter that he left out the great philosophical questions of the age – in fact, that was the point. This was all about life lived exuberantly and although Socrates said, 'The unexamined life is not worth living,' he'd never been out for a drink with Noel Gallagher. While the simplicity and instant familiarity of the tunes were a source of ready criticism, it would be time which would tell their appeal. The primal stomp of 'Rock'n'Roll Star' and 'Live Forever' would hold up for years. But even at the time Gallagher was convinced of the album's longevity. It was sometimes dismissed as mere bragging when he said, 'In 20 years' time people will buy the album and listen to it for what it is. They won't listen to it because we were rock'n'roll or something like that. That's what matters.'

Almost 20 years later his words seemed less like a daring statement of intent and more like a matter of general agreement. In 2006 the album was voted the best of all time by some 40,000 readers of a chart book and NME.com, with follow-up *(What's the Story?) Morning Glory* at No 5. That same all-time Top 20 was notable for featuring no other albums by Brit Pop era bands, unless you wanted to include Radiohead (*OK Computer, The Bends*) or the Stone

Roses' debut, neither of which seemed to fit comfortably into that genre.

Few other Oasis albums would approach *Definitely Maybe* in terms of relentless energy and lack of clutter. It was direct. Gallagher's astute appropriation of his influences meant that his own songs had a similar quality of timelessness, a Stooges-like urgency which never aged. Another hint of Gallagher's influences was to be found on the cover in the form of Burt Bacharach, whose picture leaned against the sofa on the left. Within two years Gallagher would be performing his 'This Guy's in Love with You' on stage with Bacharach himself in London. And there was Noel Gallagher himself on the cover of *Definitely Maybe*, stood in the centre, holding a large globe in his hand and staring down the viewer. 'Nice planet,' he seemed to be saying. 'I'll take it.' Liam measured his length on the floor and ignored the hubris, a glass of wine by his head.

Definitely Maybe came in at UK No 1, its success in part down to Creation's then-limited resources. MD Tim Abbot advertised in non-traditional areas for music like football match programmes. The music press were enthusiastic, the *NME*'s Keith Cameron saying, 'Noel Gallagher is a pop craftsman in the classic tradition and a master of his trade. Of his generation, probably only Kurt Cobain wielded the manipulative power of melody better, and you can't imagine Noel having many guilt pangs about whether or not "Live Forever" was just that little bit too perfect.'

It almost already didn't really matter what the press

thought. Like subsequent Oasis albums, *Definitely Maybe* would, to all intents and purposes, be critic-proof, as Gallagher's raging self-belief and back-to-basics approach touched so many collective reference points with his audience.

'Of course. Too right ... I'm glad to be old school and I'm glad I've got me values,' he told *NME*. 'I'm glad I've got them ideals and they were taught me by fucking Bob Marley and John Lennon and John Lydon and Paul Weller and Morrissey and Marr and people like that.' Following generations of bands would then have to define themselves against Oasis. Acts like Razorlight would go the guitar anthem route with songs like 2006's 'America', while Arctic Monkeys supplied the gritty lyrics and the Libertines did the chaotic front section routine with Pete Doherty and Carl Barat filling in the roles of brothers. It would all have its roots in the songbook that Gallagher was beginning to fill up with Oasis's debut.

The towering achievement didn't, however, have a noticeably beneficial effect on the brothers' relationship. Noel Gallagher would years later put the start of their arguments down to this first taste of getting somewhere. Perhaps their mother's attitude was the best response. Peggy had long followed a policy of strict non-interventionism. While she wanted nothing more than for the boys to get on together, she took infinite pains to make sure that she didn't take one side over another. Her role was not so much peacemaker but impartial referee, though it would take more than that to resolve their differences. Nobody else could help them find equilibrium and the pressures of success did little to make that seem more likely.

With the brothers beginning to wonder where the success left their own positions, triumphant Oasis set out to conquer America in September, though the reception could never match up to the hysteria at home. They made up for it with their own and very public falling out. For the first time, Noel walked out on the band and went off for a week. He had to be tracked down by Creation MD Tim Abbot and persuaded not to split the band for good. As with everything to do with their intricate, strange relationship, what really happened – or at least what prompted Noel to walk away – was not clear. Shortly afterwards, the *NME* reported him saying, 'If you find out what happened, you'll have the greatest story ever. You will know everything.' The strain was real, but for the audience back home the tales of brotherly discord were more exciting and, as with the much publicised fights earlier in the year, made them seem more attractive than a smoothly professional tour could ever have done. It was only away from the difficulties in the US and seeing how popular the band were back in the UK, with sold out gigs awaiting, that Gallagher felt more positive about the future.

With his poise recovered, Gallagher showed again how he could be a master at putting a good spin on any calamity that might befall the band. He would hijack interviews to make his experience of being a rising star seem as exciting to readers as it was for him. Interviewers would struggle to convey the sheer entertainment of having him as a subject. They would often have to put in stage directions to show how he did accents and wicked impersonations of fellow stars or stood up mid-chat to act out scenarios and give his anecdotes maximum impact. Gallagher might have been unimpressed by many aspects of the music industry, but he was never cool about the fundamental greatness of being a musician for a living .Yet despite his skill with the press, he never felt the need to alter how his image was portrayed. 'We've always been so-called bad boys of English rock,' he said in 1997. They were, he explained, the ones known for rude hand gestures and 'saying "cunt" in interviews ... I'm not bothered about it though.'

No subject was off limits as the years passed and Gallagher could usually rely on his brother to chip in at decisive moments on the occasions when they did joint interviews. Even in the month of the attacks on the World Trade Center of 2001, as they were absorbing the significance, the Bin Laden assault was assimilated into one of Gallagher's by then trademark *NME* rants. It began with an innocuous comment on musical ability. 'Three chords on a guitar: now write a song. I only know 11! But I tell you what, God help you when I find the 12th! I'm telling you! And if I ever start reading fucking books? I'll take over the fucking world! It'll be me crashing into the fucking Trade towers.'

Seemingly without missing a beat, Liam improvised coverage of this event, 'You're live to CNN where Noel

Gallagher has just crashed into the new World Trade fucking office!' It was the trademark Gallagher delight in eye-catching quotes which made their interviews such good value and Noel was particularly adept at the form. Yet catch him on a more reflective day and he would be seeing both sides of a conflict – on another occasion he spoke again of the aftermath of 9/11: 'People don't actually fucking hate each other ... It's just there's extremists in that community, but there's extremists in our community – in Whitehall. It's fucking bad darts, man.'

Ranging so widely over apparently unconnected subjects in interview would become expected of Gallagher as his reputation built. He would frequently slip into those note-perfect versions of accents that he encountered in his life touring the world and he would mesmerise music journalists with weapons-grade gossip and comic stories from his encounters at the top of the music industry. He never seemed to forget where he had come from and treated his outings in the media as a cross between swapping war stories down the pub with friends and letting his fans in on massive secrets. It was harder to do than it looked – to be intimate, opinionated and hold it all together with such an immaculate sense of comic timing.

Gallagher was as down-to-earth about his new friends in the upper reaches of the music industry as he was about most things. It wouldn't be long before he was knocking about with one-time heroes like Paul Weller, but he made the name-drop sound endearingly matey. 'We hardly ever talk to each other,' he said, 'it's just drunken babble nonsense.' Yet Gallagher paid enough attention to their encounters to be able to do an exceptionally good impersonation of his drinking buddy just to ensure his stories would seem that much richer. And his casual description of the two men boozing together couldn't hide how he was just always too charismatic and aware to be the sloppy barfly he liked to suggest he was.

In another discussion about music with a journalist he gave a particularly compelling reason for not being into jazz. He had been asked about the criticism he faced in dealing only in one style of music. Not everyone could possibly like every type of music, he pointed out. And he was comfortable with that. But he had a particularly splendid reason for 'fucking hating' jazz. And another Gallagher polemic was expertly delivered. 'Jazz is four people onstage having a better time than the 400 people in the audience,' he said. 'That's what fucking jazz is. Don't get me started on classical music. Don't get me started on heavy metal. It's just bollocks.' Gallagher never seemed to be bored by conjuring inventive responses to questions, no matter how trivial or seemingly dead-end. When the internet made paying for a music an option rather than a requirement, he convinced an awe-struck writer that he was seriously considering making everything free – even the band's gigs. 'Yeah, they're free to get in – but you got to pay 75 quid to get out. That'd be great at Wembley, wouldn't it?'

Throughout his career he was never afraid to say what he

thought about other bands – to begin with it was the established acts in his sights. But as Oasis became a fixture it would be his peers who he would square up to with some pithy putdown. Yet, as he grew into the role of elder statesman of rock, he showed no sign of becoming more measured – then it would be the young hopefuls he'd light up with a Gallagher word bomb. He once related how a guitarist he insulted had said the experience had been an honour. He claimed to be incredulous that anyone would be pleased to be at the end of his barbed comments, but it was clear that he could see the funny side too. He knew that any artist would benefit from association with Noel Gallagher. Everyone won – it was good to get some Oasis-related press if you were a band on the way up and Gallagher got to show again how his passion for music remained undimmed as each new wave of bands came along.

He simply never seemed to find it hard to identify with the wide-eyed music obsessive he had been as a kid. It meant that he always seemed to know what fans wanted to hear on stage as well. Even when he was later able to afford a big country pile and required security when he went on promotional tours, Gallagher made sure that he continued to go out to see more gigs than most and was determinedly unworried about any personal risks he might run as a star.

In the aftermath of the first hit album, the music business, journalists and fans couldn't get enough of Noel Gallagher and Oasis, no matter how much they provoked. In October, the month after the difficult US tour 'Cigarettes and Alcohol' was released. The paean to hedonism with Liam's Sex Pistols snarl was the fourth single from their debut and industry logic dictated that the public would have had enough of the album by then. Instead it hit UK No 7.

For Gallagher the song was right up there with 'Rocks' by Primal Scream as a good-time classic. The comparison was apt. His Creation label mates were as influenced by classic rock and psychedelia as Gallagher's band and it would be a tie as to who had more of a reputation for hard living. Primal Scream had departed from the indie dance of 1991's *Screamadelica* and appropriated Rolling Stones-like rhythms for *Give Out But Don't Give Up*. On the rare occasions you might turn on the radio and not hear one of Oasis's singles, you'd be likely to hear 'Rocks'. The two songs, said Gallagher at the time, 'are the only youth anthems for as long as I can remember that just say, "Go out and get pissed, fall about, jump up and down in the air, listen to some music, smoke something, snort something and have a good time".' Of comparisons to glam rock classics by T Rex's Marc Bolan, Gallagher was disarmingly frank. 'It's a blues riff. He nicked it off Howlin' Wolf anyway!'

The familiarity of the tune and the straightforwardness of the lyric did nothing but strengthen the appeal of the song. It underlined how much had changed as the 1990s really got underway and the politicised 1980s receded into memory. Where once indie rock identified itself firmly with the left and activism, Noel Gallagher was saying it was okay to be indulgent, to make the best of what you've got and just have fun. And that was the message that everyone heard.

The appeal of the single might well have been in part due to its b-side. Gallagher paid almost as much attention to them as to the lead song and to albums as a whole. It was for him a throwback to a pre-CD time when singles came on vinyl and the b-side was a chance to get to know a less familiar aspect to a band. Not least with Noel Gallagher taking on lead vocals, as 'Fade Away' was included with 'Cigarettes & Alcohol', a driving track which could easily have made it onto the album itself. As if acknowledging that, Gallagher would later rework it for *Help!*, the War Child charity album the following year.

Fans were already looking forward to the next instalment in the story as Oasis moved inexorably centre stage in the UK. They were achieving that rare feat of crossing over from the world of the indie rocker to mainstream success but without losing the edge which had made them the darlings of the music press – particularly the *NME*. *(What's the Story?) Morning Glory* wouldn't disappoint, but before that there was a completely new song in the run-up to Christmas.

'Whatever' was business as usual for Oasis, in its lyrics of free-floating positivity and vaguely threatening sense of personal entitlement. But this time the inevitable strumalong intro heralded something of an innovation for the band in the shape of a sizeable string section, a nod to another great tradition in English pop. 'Whatever' made it to UK No 3 and seemed to underline the connection to the lineage of the Beatles which Gallagher kept in the minds of the press, even when he was purporting to establish some distance from it. In one article he agreed that his brother was very keen on identifying himself with John Lennon, but he himself had a more balanced view. Other members of the band, he said, believed 'Abbey Road is special because of the Beatles. I think it's a studio with shit gear in it.'

The b-side to 'Whatever', 'Half the World Away', later became the theme to *The Royle Family*. As a result it became impossible after 1998 to hear the song without thinking of the Caroline Aherne and Craig Cash sitcom. Perhaps because, like Noel Gallagher, it was straightforward, unapologetically northern and utterly deadpan. The Royles were to comedy what the Gallagher brothers were to rock music. Here was a family who did what anyone might recognise – bicker, sit around watching telly and drink tea. And it was around the telly that their personal dramas unfolded and that invested the Ricky Tomlinson-led cast with genuine sympathy and warmth. For now, Gallagher's own vocals were tucked away on b-sides, but the show would give the song and his voice new prominence.

The single was also the source of another legal battle when Neil Innes, former member of 1960s' satirical band the Bonzo Dog Doo Dah Band, successfully brought an action over similarities between sections of the song and his 'How Sweet to be an Idiot'. Ironically, Innes, along with former Monty Python member Eric Idle, had also been behind the Rutles, as much a tribute to as it was a pastiche of the Beatles. They had even made a fake rockumentary of the Rutles in the 1970s, *All You Need is Cash*. In some respects, Innes and Gallagher were doing similar things in acknowledging the pervasive influences of acts who had gone before. It was just easier to accept when it came with a laugh.

But rather than hinder the progress of Oasis the legal actions, like the arguments between the brothers themselves, served to assist the myth of the band and the legend of Noel Gallagher as the ultimate maverick star. The Oasis machine seemed to be fuelled rather than derailed by association with controversy. The band themselves didn't seem to mind at all. They would never struggle with being in the limelight like others who came to sit at the top table of music by the mid-1990s. Acts like Elastica, whose eponymous 1995 album would define much of what would be Brit Pop, took five years to follow it up. Even brash Blur seemed to be a bit disorientated by the bright lights. Pulp took three years to follow *Different Class* and the very title of 1998's *This is Hardcore* suggested that, having once made the case for Common People being allowed to join pop's elite, the experience didn't make Jarvis Cocker as cheerful as he might have expected.

Noel Gallagher, by contrast, loved it. He would party solidly for the next three or four years. Like his Sheffield contemporaries, he had endured enough anonymity for the first quarter of a century of his life and he inhaled deeply when he got a whiff of good times. And if he had to sacrifice some privacy in the process he showed no sign of being troubled by it. Or at least very little. Asked by the *NME* what the non-Gallaghers in the band were like he said, 'Anonymous. Lucky bastards.' But even that sounded light-hearted.

At the centre of a now famous family, Peggy Gallagher remained entirely unchanged by the success of her sons, not even leaving the council house she had occupied since leaving her husband. The youngest Gallagher would offer to buy her a new place around the village of Alderley Edge, some ten miles south of Manchester, but she was not one to give up what she knew. She had her routines, her circle of friends, sisters and grandchildren and she had never looked for anything else. Her one concession to the excesses of the rock'n'roll lifestyle was a new front garden gate to replace an original which had squeaked for years. And, with the addition of a house number in gold, that was as close to superstardom as Mrs Gallagher cared to go.

It had been an extraordinary year by any standards and on 29 December 1994, Oasis played in Brighton, supported by another Creation band, Ride (whose co-founder was future Oasis friend and member Andy Bell) and the La's, with a promotional poster depicting a Parka-ed, mono-browed cartoon figure riding an amusement arcade motorbike. Oasis didn't need any gimmicks now – any tour they announced would inevitably sell out. Tomorrow belonged to Oasis – and to Noel Gallagher.

CHAPTER 5

ROUND
ARE WAY

'CAN YOU PUT THE LIGHTERS AWAY?
YOU'RE NOT AT AN ELTON JOHN GIG.'
NOEL GALLAGHER INTRODUCING HIS
ACOUSTIC 'WONDERWALL', EARLS COURT, 1995

London was the place that Noel Gallagher, one of the world's most famous Mancunians and surely its most renowned Man City fan, now called home. While every interview he conducted and the attitude of each song he wrote underlined his roots, he had the chameleon nature of many successful artists. *Definitely Maybe* had established his group as stars and the centre of the music business was still the capital. It simply made sense for him to be in the city. But the ease with which he took to the life underlined how far he was prepared to travel from his Burnage upbringing. And the capital city was good to creative people like that. It could absorb people from anywhere and they didn't need to feel they had to behave like natives and yet they could be absorbed into its indefinable character.

Gallagher was also putting down roots in his personal life which would seal his status as a long-term resident of the south. Having split from long-term girlfriend Louise Jones in 1994, Gallagher had been introduced to Meg Mathews. Their contact came through Meg's flatmate, MTV Europe presenter and singer Rebecca De Ruvo. Within the year Gallagher and Mathews were sharing a flat in Camden Town's Albert Street, not far from the Good Mixer pub which would in time come to be known as the operational headquarters for Brit Pop.

Meg Mathews, like Gallagher, came from a working class background. Her father was a carpenter from Liverpool and her mother was a secretary. Born a year before Gallagher, Mathews grew up in Guernsey and South Africa and was sent to boarding school in Banbury, Oxfordshire. Here, she met future director Guy Ritchie and his sister Tabitha. She was also, she said, expelled from the school for being 'boy mad'. She hitchhiked to London and her work included being personal assistant to Betty Boo who would be known for her 1990 hit 'Doin' the Do'. Mathews was glamorous and attractive and complemented Gallagher. She knew how to negotiate her away around the trendiest nooks and crannies to which he was increasingly being invited.

The beginning of 1995 for Oasis had been spent touring North America. 'Live Forever', which had done so well for the band in the UK the previous year, was released in the

US during the tour and it was then that the hard work slogging around the massive distances over the Atlantic paid off. The song went higher than any Oasis track had done in either the UK or the US, hitting No 2 in the modern rock chart. MTV had featured a new US video intercut with photos of the band's various influences and the result was this most English of bands was becoming a viable international proposition. The video imagery was effective if even less subtle than the lyrics – at one point a *Sun* front page flashed up featuring the headline SID VICIOUS DEAD, a reminder where none was needed that the former Sex Pistols bassist discovered he wouldn't live forever when he was in New York.

Suddenly the reported rows that had marred the previous September's US tour faded into insignificance. Back then many had dismissed Gallagher's claims of imminent greatness. Comparisons with the Beatles only really held up if he was to emulate his '60s heroes and crack the States. Now Oasis seemed to be on the verge of doing just that, although there were still bumps along the way. On 20 March in Michigan's Orbit Room Liam got hit by one of the flying objects which the laddish audiences they attracted insisted on throwing the band's way and he walked off early in the set. Once again it was left to his brother to carry the rest of the show and iconic songs such as 'Cigarettes & Alcohol' and 'Supersonic'.

While the US soaked up the reputation of Oasis, back home it was Blur who beat them to the Best Album award

at the Brits in February for *Parklife* and also scooped Best
Group and Best Single for the single 'Parklife' ('Girls &
Boys' had also been among the nominations against
'Whatever'). Blur won four awards in total, but Oasis did
take Best British Newcomer, fighting off competition from
Ant & Dec – then trading under the name PJ & Duncan –
as well as Portishead and Echobelly. The *NME* Brat Awards
also featured a strong showing by Blur and Oasis as well as
Gene. It was here that relations soured with Blur as Liam
told Damon Albarn either that his band were shit or were
full of shit – reports differed. In any event, it was the start of
the year in which British pop shuffled out of the music
papers and took up residence in the tabloids as the soap
opera Brit Pop.

The awards seemed to show that Oasis were not quite yet
making good on the promise they had shown with their
debut. But Gallagher hadn't let the focus on cracking the
US interrupt his creative flow – there would be little let up
in his activities, whether touring, writing or partying, until
well after *Be Here Now*. Now, with astonishing rapidity,
he was planning to go back into the studio to kick off
recording sessions early in the year. It had taken Blur three
albums to approach the level of recognition that he was
aiming for with two – and there was far more equality of
musical input from the four members of Blur.

Owen Morris returned with Oasis to act as producer.
Serving to underline the link between Gallagher and the
Verve's Richard Ashcroft, Morris had spent the previous

few months working on *A Northern Soul*. He'd been recommended to Ashcroft in the first place by an impressed Noel Gallagher as much for how well he fitted in with the character of the band as for his technical abilities. The first track to come out of the sessions was 'Some Might Say', recorded at Loco Studios in Wales in February, though it had to be redone when Gallagher and Morris decided it was a bit too fast.

'The demo has got a great groove on it, proper, slow Stonesy sort of groove, it's a lot slower,' said Morris. 'But what happens when Oasis get in the studio is that Noel is all hyped up and he starts playing doubly fast.' Such was the dedication to their work that the decision to record again was made after everyone else had gone to bed, but the rest of the group were immediately awoken and another take made. This too proved to have problems and in the free-wheeling exuberance of the session nobody noticed until Morris got to finalising the song. The sheer fun of working with Oasis came through in his memories of working on what would be the first single from an album that had otherwise yet to be recorded. 'I mixed it ["Some Might Say"] on three separate occasions,' he said, 'finally putting on all the delays and chaos in an attempt to hide the mistakes. I still love "Some Might Say". It's one of my favourite Noel songs, and I like the sheer chaos of the recording. The song overcame everything.'

On 22 April, just days before the single's release, Oasis played a show in Sheffield, their first arena date, supported by local hopefuls Pulp. Gallagher had instigated a solo portion of the show which he would use to play such numbers as 'Sad Song' as well as b-sides. 'Gonna play a brand new one,' he said at one point in this intimate slot, adding, 'I only wrote it on Tuesday. So no one's heard this before. This is for [Lee] Mavers, by the way. You've not heard this one yet, mate. I haven't got a title for it either.' And then he started strumming. Gallagher's regard for the La's legendarily perfectionist frontman was no secret. He would one day tell Radio 1, 'There's only one songwriter in this country who scares me and that is Lee Mavers.' But that night he had something to rival any other composer. It sounded marvellously complete even with only Gallagher and his guitar and if it wasn't named at that point it only needed a title to finish 'Don't Look Back in Anger'. Even Paul Weller might have been impressed by this – when Gallagher had played him 'Roll With It' in the run up to recording the new Oasis album, Weller had countered with stronger extracts from *Stanley Road*, which would be released early in the summer. Their session inspired Gallagher to take his own writing further, but the Sheffield gig showed how, when things were going well, his biggest songs seemed to arrive almost fully formed.

The 'Don't Look Back in Anger' chord progression had already been in place two days earlier, at a soundcheck for a gig the band were doing with the Verve in Paris. The words, again, were the last thing to come. Liam asked about the line mentioning Sally and it was as if that provided all the inspiration Noel needed to complete the lyrics. Keeping it in the family, Noel thought back to his childhood when Peggy Gallagher would get all three brothers to pose for their annual Christmas photograph to be sent to their grandmother in Ireland. They'd be instructed to stand by the fireplace and that's when there would be a particular pre-photo look they'd be firmly instructed to take off their faces. The final song was one that was so completely owned by Noel that whenever he got to singing it live, Liam would walk off the stage.

As 'Some Might Say' was being issued, there were tensions within Oasis which were coming to a head. It was perhaps inevitable that as they were approaching fame, the pressures on the personnel would be at their greatest. For some time the relationship with drummer Tony McCarroll hadn't been good. As 'Some Might Say' confirmed what everyone already knew about the potential for the band and gave them their first UK No 1, it was announced that he was no longer part of Oasis. A court case followed in 1999 and McCarroll accepted an out-of-court settlement.

Paul Weller's drummer Steve White had a brother, Alan, in the same trade and from Gallagher's friendship came the recommendation that he fill the vacancy. Although he had been drumming for years, he hadn't had experience of playing with anyone as big as Oasis. But there was no time for a gentle induction with a new single to promote and he ended up making his debut with 'Some Might Say' on *Top of the Pops*.

He had arrived in time for a triumphant performance and the ultimate vindication of everything Gallagher had believed he and his band were capable of, but there were further treats in store for fans. Once again paying attention to b-sides, 'Acquiesce' from 'Some Might Say' became a live favourite – it had been a strong contender for single in its own right. The band had played it on *The White Room*, a Channel 4 music programme, in April. The show treated its musicians seriously and it was another solo platform for Gallagher as he was also joined by Paul Weller who provided provide electric piano for a version of another 'Some Might Say' b-side song, 'Talk Tonight'. Weller's appearance was a measure of the respect as a writer that Gallagher was beginning to attract.

Much less than a year had elapsed since *Definitely Maybe* had hit UK No 1 but, with a tour including a headlining slot in Glastonbury looming, the band returned to Wales for the second time to do the main sessions for the album. They had a few weeks booked at Rockfield Studios in Monmouth. Rockfield had the sort of distinguished history of patrons which would have appealed to Gallagher's sense of his place among the greats, from Queen and Black Sabbath to the Damned and Adam and the Ants. And Simple Minds. No demos of the songs had been made and, as Gallagher later remembered it, nobody from Creation had heard what they were about to commit their resources to recording. It didn't seem to matter.

'The session was the best, easiest, least fraught, most happily creative time I've ever had in a recording studio,' said Owen Morris. 'I honestly believe that the lack of any badness and only good intent and love from everyone involved is a very important part of why ...*Morning Glory* is liked by so many people. I believe people can feel and hear when music is dishonest and motivated by the wrong reasons. ...*Morning Glory*, for all its imperfection and flaws, is dripping with love and happiness.'

Over the years, Gallagher would get the band to record b-sides when they first went into the studio, particularly when they hadn't been recording for a while, just to remind themselves of how they did their thing. With ...*Morning Glory*, the band barely needed to ease themselves back into work, so constantly were they touring and so recent was their last session. But Gallagher was determined not simply to repeat his formula – the new album was going to be a more ambitious affair.

The debut had been characterised by a basic approach, an all-out attack of guitars. 'The sound of *Definitely Maybe* was a bit one-dimension,' said Gallagher. 'Everything was the same tone – whack it up to ten and off we go.' This time around more tracks were layered. The different approach came alongside the jazzier edge to the drumming contributed by new recruit Alan White and the result was an expansive, less urgent sound than before, with the biggest numbers being those with elements of ballads about them. For every 'Roll With It' there was a 'Don't Look Back in Anger' or even a 'Cast No Shadow'. And the speed of the sessions was an impressive indication of the commitment to realising Gallagher's ambition, the band getting down something like a track a day until disagreements between the brothers led to an unexpected halt.

'Noel knew exactly where he was with his songs,' said Morris. 'Big choruses that everyone wanted to sing along to. That was fundamentally it.' It was this uncompromising vision which fostered a perception of the band that had Gallagher as somewhat distanced from the passion of making music. He was in creative control of Oasis and that could be interpreted as him being somehow detached from the raw spirit of the band embodied by his brother. Noel would even sometimes play other instruments in the recording sessions, so clear was his sense of how he wanted things to sound and so overriding was his impatience to get what was in his head down as quickly as possible. Studio time could be minimised as Gallagher knew the arrangements he wanted. There was even a concept – of sorts. If *Definitely Maybe* had been about dreaming of rock'n'roll, ...*Morning Glory* was about living it. 'Which probably sounds like an arse thing to say,' said Gallagher, 'but it's true.'

One of the more entertaining ideas was to record guitar for 'Wonderwall' with Noel and guitar perched on an actual wall in the rural studio. He played up the gag in later interviews, 'So I climb up this massive great wall and I'm shitting myself, and there's all this recording equipment out in the yard and all these geese and sheep and cows looking through the fence, going, "Fucking hell, look at him!"'

More seriously, Gallagher wanted to take the lead vocal for 'Don't Look Back in Anger' and the trade-off was that Liam would do 'Wonderwall'. But Noel taking such a juicy lead added a new dynamic to their relationship and whenever that most delicate of working dynamics in Oasis was altered at any point in their career there was always the potential for a new fault line to open up. Yet when the sparks flew between the brothers and, to a lesser extent, the rest of the band, that was when the chemistry of the band happened. Explosive liquids sloshed together, the place lit up and a natural force was unleashed. It was as much true in the studio as on stage and it was something that maybe only brothers could replicate. 'When I'm trying to get Liam to sing something in the correct manner and he's just not gonna do it, because he's a stubborn little cunt,' said Gallagher, 'I'll be like, "I'll sing it then." It's amazing how you get it in one take after that.'

This time, after a particularly difficult night, the band ended up taking an enforced break from recording. Yet when Noel was ready to resume it was as if nothing had happened. Such strains on their partnership as siblings must have been contributing to the problems they would encounter working together in the future, but nobody in Oasis was thinking about the future. Not when everything was going so well and when Gallagher's writing seemed to be virtually effortless. The songs were pouring out of him: returning on the train to the studio, Gallagher wrote 'Cast No Shadow', the song he dedicated to Richard Ashcroft.

A Northern Soul came out that summer and while Oasis overshadowed them commercially, Gallagher was open about his admiration for their work. Not that he needed to see them as rivals when he had so few problems with his own creativity.

'The freakiest thing,' Owen Morris later wrote, 'was that, unlike most guitarists who rely on "capturing the moment" and "getting in the vibe", Noel can just turn it on, stone-cold sober in the middle of the afternoon. He doesn't need to get off his head and wait for the magic to happen, he just does it. He can turn it on. It comes seemingly without him trying too hard.' Gallagher fizzed with ideas for the guitar parts, coming up with different lines and feedback parts which transformed songs at a stroke.

Such was the pace of life that the band began what would be more than a hundred dates touring the world in support of the *(What's the Story?) Morning Glory* while work on it continued. Alan White's live debut with the band came at the Bath Pavilion on 22 June. A far more prestigious slot followed the next day as Oasis headlined the Friday night at Glastonbury. They had first appeared the previous year when they had been no less confident. Emily Eavis, daughter of the festival's founder, later told *Guardian* music writer Alexis Petridis: 'It's really rare that you put a band on that early and they fill the stage with such potential and arrogance. You normally see shy indie bands, terrified because it's their first Glastonbury. Everyone was really taken by how assured they were.'

Yet their appearance in 1995 was overshadowed by Pulp, who owned Glastonbury that year. While Pulp had not yet had great recognition in their long career, they were consistent in their output and *Different Class*, which would be released in the autumn, had already set out their claim for being Brit Pop's court jesters with the single 'Common People' and 'Mis-Shapes' / 'Sorted for Es and Wizz' to follow later in the year. They were filling in at Glastonbury for a Mani-less Stone Roses, who had cancelled after John Squire had a cycling accident.

The Stone Roses had received a mixed response to *Second Coming* at the end of the previous year and now it seemed that Oasis were stepping into the space they had vacated. And part of the urgency to follow up *Definitely Maybe* might well have come from Gallagher's determination not to let momentum dissipate as the Stone Roses had. If anything, Oasis were at the opposite end of the scale – everything was going their way and they could probably have afforded to have taken things a little slower – but that was not Gallagher's way when there was still too much to be done. By spring of 1996 the Stone Roses would split and the promise they had held out at the beginning of the decade would finally disappear for good.

Take That would split the same year, but it had been during the 1995 Glastonbury that the ultimate boy band had shown signs of the wheels coming off their finely-honed machine. The festival had been notable also for the Oasis-wooing of Robbie Williams, doing his best to achieve escape velocity from Take That with antics that contravened their strictly wholesome ethos. Robbie Williams was in some ways the ideal Oasis fan – excitable and inspired by the rock'n'roll lifestyle they embodied. But Gallagher barely blinked and the friendship wasn't lasting as Robbie Williams went his own way. Gallagher was so single-minded in his goal of getting Oasis to be the biggest band in the world that events of the size of Glastonbury and teen idols wanting to be his mate were interludes on the road to total domination.

The scale of the operation had got to the point where other people around the band had to take more responsibility for planning and executing strategy. Gallagher still retained overall control but they had come so far since the early days when it had just been him making the phone calls to book gigs and get his band noticed. As vital as the changes were, they meant the character of what drove the band was altered, but it would take time for the differences to be felt, particularly as Gallagher was never given a period of reflection. Instead touring continued simultaneously with the final elements for the album being added in the studio back in London. Further cementing his friendship with Gallagher, Paul Weller turned up to return the favour done for him earlier in the year when Gallagher had played on his version of 'I Walk on Gilded Splinters'. Weller added guitar to 'Champagne Supernova' and 'The Swamp Song'. He recorded his parts in an easy afternoon.

'Noel was like a pig in shit that day,' said Owen Morris,

who had finalised the mixes by July. The mastering was done extra loud, setting a benchmark for the industry. At the time it all seemed, like so much around Oasis, like it was a bit over the top. Soon enough though, everybody would be doing their albums the same way.

The release of the album would be, as was customary, heralded by the release of a single, but the usually routine question of its schedule became unexpectedly dramatic. Gallagher might have always firmly believed his band would be talked about throughout the land and he might even have been resigned to it being through tabloid shock stories. But he would hardly have thought that Oasis and Blur would end up not just making headlines but becoming the news itself simply because of a clashing release date. 'Roll With It' was set to hit the shops on 14 August, with Blur's 'Country House' slated for two weeks later. But amid a war of words, they both ended up coming out on 7 August. The reasoning depended on who you believed – one side had it that Blur, perhaps Damon Albarn himself, were supposed to have wanted to get some publicity by going up against Oasis. Otherwise Blur's record company had become nervous because Oasis were having too long a lead-in time for their October album. The truth was ultimately unimportant when the result was that the charts stopped being the preserve of the music press and became the harbinger of a full-blown cultural earthquake. This was to be a good, old-fashioned punch-up and even those who had never heard a song by Oasis or Blur could follow that one when the duel made the headlines in national TV news. Older viewers remembered the battles between the Rolling Stones and the Beatles – then, as this time around, largely manufactured by the media – and for the first time in years the charts mattered.

The quality of the songs wasn't the major part of the equation. This was the music business equivalent of a derby and at the time when fair weather sporting fans everywhere were declaring their undying love for a major team, having never previously reported ever seeing a game, now everyone in the country had to pick a side. To make it even easier for the headline writers, the two musical teams couldn't have been more clearly cast.

Blur were the chirpy underdogs. Arty, southern contenders, they enthusiastically played up their roles. The 'Country House' video was directed by Damien Hirst, king of the Young British Artists, another tabloid staple of the mid-1990s and as simultaneously hyped and reviled by the media as anything in the music industry. Bridging the gap with Brit Pop was the clip's star – comedian, actor and London scenester Keith Allen. He was ably supported by the likes of alternative comedian Matt Lucas. The tumbling jauntiness of the song's bassline set 'Country House' out as the epitome of cheeky London attitude. Damon Albarn may not have actually sung, 'Have a banana,' but the package exuded humour and the attitude of the new wave of alternative comedians who were, along with the YBAs and Brit Pop, the defining cultural onslaught of the 1990s.

Moving the single had been a great PR stunt even if it hadn't been intended that way.

In a way, it left Gallagher slightly wrong-footed. Oasis had nowhere to go but to take the position of dour northerners. They had to be the chippy gatecrashers even though 'Roll With It' was the more innocent of the tracks, the more positive in its message. But somehow a lack of artifice translated into a lack of sophistication in the way the two acts were portrayed. Amid claims that 'Country House' coming on two CDs, each with different bonus tracks, and a misprinted barcode on 'Roll With It' had cost Oasis precious sales, their video was a more straightforward performance shoot. And there were probably stronger songs on the album. 'Roll With It' said nothing that earlier singles hadn't, but nevertheless it was impressive in having been recorded in one take and the energy was obvious from the moment that Liam laid into his brother's opening lyric. The chorus opened the track and every line felt like a mini-anthem, but ultimately the verses just didn't build on the opener in the same way. Perhaps unfairly, Gallagher's song was compared to Status Quo for the chugalong nature of the track, though b-sides 'Rocking' Chair' and 'It's Better People' had more intriguing arrangements.

Oasis lost the initial scramble to Blur by a relatively low 58,000. A track along the lines of 'Some Might Say' would have provided a more solid opposition, yet neither band exactly needed to try too hard with all the attendant publicity. Later Gallagher would say that he didn't even like the Oasis effort – 'I can't stand it, right?' – but by that point either band could have released a test tone single and it would have charted. As it was, 'Roll With It' became an immediate live staple and, like it or not, Gallagher would regularly have a stadium full of fans enthusiastically bouncing along to it. 'Country House' had shifted 274,000 to 216,000 for 'Roll With It' in the first week – in normal circumstances, none too shabby a result for either camp. Indeed, by 2011, the Oasis single had sold almost half a million copies. But in mid-1995, in the heat of the moment, with all that national news coverage, the bickering between the two groups became something rather more deeply-felt.

The battle's lowest point came in September with an interview in the *Observer* with Miranda Sawyer. It was a throwaway line which became big news when Gallagher was quoted as saying he hated 'them two' – Damon Albarn and bassist Alex James and that he hoped they'd catch AIDS and die. But Gallagher was nothing if not instinctively attuned to the media and he would have been immediately aware of how damaging that would be. A formal apology soon appeared in a letter to the *Melody Maker*. 'The off-the-cuff remark was made last month at the height of a "war of words" between both bands, and it must have been the 50th time during that interview that I was pressed to give an opinion of Blur. As soon as I said it, I realised it was an insensitive thing to say, as AIDS is no joking matter and immediately retracted the comment but was horrified to pick up the *Observer* and find the journalist concerned chose to still run with it.'Yet few newspapers would have been able to put such a comment to one side. It was always inevitable that such a controversial statement from someone so prominent and outspoken as Noel Gallagher would be printed. He concluded, 'Although not being a fan of their music, I wish both Damon and Alex a long and healthy life.'

Despite the apology, the comment would continue to be thrown back at Gallagher for years, though it was hardly representative of him as a person. Even at his most uncompromising, there was more usually intelligence and humour behind his comments, never more so than when he was directing his deadpan opinion at artists who liked to be experimental. Radiohead remained the perennial target throughout Oasis's long career. He never seemed to cease to be both fascinated and yet dismissive of the directions they would take. 'Come on, *In Rainbows*?' he said of their 2007 album. 'What the fuck does that mean? Can you be in a rainbow? All the action is supposed to be at the end of the rainbow, isn't it? Maybe that's where Radiohead are fucking going wrong. Thom [Yorke] has led them into the rainbow, when all the laughs and the good times are at the end. That's why you're in pain, lads.'

Following the Brit Pop singles battle, Gallagher and Damon Albarn didn't cross paths for so long that, as is sometimes the way with these things, when they did finally get together it was hard to remember what the problem had been. By the time of the Brits in 2012 they were friends, having met a while previously in a Mayfair nightclub.

Albarn said, 'What normally happened in that situation was we had a way of looking a certain way and walking past. It was like a code. But we broke the code that night, instantly. We looked at each other and said, "Hello", and it made all the difference.' And then Albarn added something of Noel that it would have been inconceivable he might have ever thought in 1995. 'A lovely man.' Gallagher reported feeling the same following their encounter.

'It was a great relief,' he said. 'I'm glad I've seen him and shook his hand and apologised for all the shit.' Though there had been bad feeling between their gangs, the truth had always been that more united Blur and Oasis than separated them. Both bands were living a life faster and wilder than most of the rest of the passengers on the ship that was soon to be named Cool Britannia. And both Albarn and Gallagher themselves were driven figures. Noel Gallagher might not end up doing the operas and the cartoon bands, but each of them had a very distinct vision of what their music should be like and the strength to carry it through. In 1995, when they were young and locking antlers, it wasn't even certain that they would sustain careers in music for as long as they have done. For a while they were all that mattered in music and it always seemed it was burning too bright to last.

But as with the copyright cases and the endless reports of the latest tour outrage, Oasis were too much of a juggernaut now for Gallagher to suffer lasting damage from the criticism that resulted from the media spats. If anything, it all contributed to their image as the bad boys of pop. The attendant publicity had done more for all concerned than any number of good reviews – the same applied not only to Blur but was a boost to any artist who might be lumped in with what was being called Brit Pop. It helped if the act in question had a one word name and also if those were more usually reserved for clothing materials – Pulp, Suede, Denim and, drawing the threads together, Menswear. The unlikeliest of bands could come out from under the music press and find themselves earning national coverage.

Gallagher might not have needed to make amends in such a climate but he did give his time to charity War Child's album *Help!* which came out in early September. He took his place in the Smokin' Mojo Filters supergroup, whose other members included Paul Weller and who recorded a cover of the Beatles' 'Come Together' with Paul McCartney. The profits from the album were in a large part directed to the children who suffered as a result of the Balkan conflict which followed the breakup of communist Yugoslavia in 1992. In the years after Live Aid it was these kind of events which more often bought different musicians together, particularly as pop was otherwise becoming increasingly depoliticised. The charity show and album remained as the main way artists who were enjoying success could make a difference. The War Child line-up was a snapshot of leading UK artists who were still clinging on to indie-hood, albeit tenuously in many cases. The Stone Roses, Suede, Blur, Radiohead and even the Stereo MCs recorded their contributions on 4 September, it was mixed the next day and in the shops by 9 September. Gallagher would have approved of the inspiration coming from John Lennon's 'Instant Karma! (We All Shine On)', having already used the 'shine' imagery many times in his lyrics for Liam to shred to satisfying effect. But the Lennon influence this time around referred to the timing of 'Instant Karma...', as he was reported to have said of the song that he completed it even faster than the War Child album. 'I wrote it for breakfast, recorded it for lunch and we're putting it out for dinner.'

Oasis themselves contributed a version of 'Fade Away', first recorded for the b-side of 'Cigarettes & Alcohol'. This time around the song was credited to 'Oasis and friends' – who included actor Johnny Depp. The brief collaboration was an indication of the rarefied circles in which Gallagher now moved, though it wasn't just a celeb turn, with Depp well-known as an accomplished musician and it wouldn't be the last time that Gallagher and Depp played together.

The main attraction remained *(What's the Story?) Morning Glory* and it was inevitable that when it was released on 2 October it would go straight to UK No 1. By the end of its first week alone it had sold 347,000 copies. Gallagher's songs had turned around the fortunes of Creation Records and Oasis proved Alan McGee's taste in music to be impeccable. Soon the nearest thing to pass for hip in political terms, new Labour, would be knocking at his door.

While Blur had won the battle of the singles, as many commentators observed at the time, Oasis won the war of the albums. ...*Morning Glory* tracks such as 'Hello' and 'She's Electric' were throwaway, 'Digsy's Dinner'-esque romps, but there was much more of substance this time around. Not just 'Don't Look Back in Anger' but 'Cast no Shadow' and 'Some Might Say' were weightier affairs. Blur's *The Great Escape*, released in September, had hit UK No 1, but the initially gushing reception – press and fans – were not sustained. By 2007 no less a critic than Damon Albarn was saying that Blur's album had been 'a bit empty. Sometimes records are like that if you try too hard to repeat your success.' He was being hard on himself but the reach of...*Morning Glory* would prove to be astonishing. By 2010 it had sold 22 million copies worldwide, 4.3 million of them in the UK alone and the standout tracks remained live favourites, whether performed by Oasis or a solo Noel Gallagher. Kids all over the world who weren't even old enough to be in school when the songs were first written would be singing along with them.

Yet as much as Gallagher talked his band up at the time, the hand of history on his shoulder was by no means a given at the time, with mixed reviews. 'Definitely nearly,' said *Select*. The second release, they said, '*is* a great album: just not as great as the last one.' And David Stubbs wrote in *Melody Maker* – never as much Gallagher's natural home as its upstart rival the *NME* – 'On this evidence, Oasis are a limited band.' And yet, in the *Independent*, Andy Gill presciently noted how the album divided neatly 'into the guitar-rock of their debut and a more pensive ballad direction, which in songs like "Don't Look Back in Anger" and "Cast No Shadow" speaks loudly of melancholy and alienation.' The US had warmed to the band and the album would do much to establish a foothold there. It was 'more than a natural progression; it's a bold leap forward that displays significant musical and personal growth,' said *Rolling Stone*, also not always a natural cheerleader for Oasis 'not to mention a far greater familiarity with the Fab Four's back catalogue.'

By May 2012 a chart of the UK's bestselling albums of all time had *...Morning Glory* at No 4. It placed Oasis just below Abba's greatest hits, *Gold*, and above *21* by Adele, who shared more in common with Gallagher than a Top 5 chart position. Both these seemingly very different artists specialised in music that seemed straightforward and immediately recognisable. They didn't try to break new ground, but they both had an innate gift for entertaining. Their main difference was that at Adele's age, Noel Gallagher was showing no signs of wanting to be a solo artist, although as the sole writer in the band he had many of the same pressures. There would be one more album before he was freed from the responsibility of coming up with the songs alone and *(What's The Story?) Morning Glory* would be a difficult feat to top. It 'cast such a shadow over us,' Gallagher later said. When it came to getting back in the studio, an increasingly large number of people would be looking at him to come up with the goods so they could get on with their job.

'Wonderwall' reached only UK No 2 on its release at the end of October, but became something of a template Oasis song in the public imagination. The one to feature Liam's singing after Noel swapped 'Don't Look Back in Anger' with him, it was widely assumed to be about Meg Mathews, something which Gallagher had said himself at the time. When the couple split up, he would later say that it was a more generalised lyric about the importance of true friendship. But for a song that for many defined that period of Oasis, it proved frustratingly elusive out of the studio. Gallagher was always striving to match the recorded quality of the song when they took it to the fans. 'We've never got it right,' he said as late as 2008. 'It's too slow or too fast. I think Ryan Adams is the only person who ever got that song right. I'd love to do the Ryan Adams version, but in front of 60,000 Oasis fans that wouldn't be possible.' So ubiquitous was the song, with its football chant chorus and that Gallagher quality of instant familiarity, that it seemed to have been UK No 1. Even Gallagher himself noted, 'We were getting sick of hearing "Wonderwall" every two minutes on the radio.'

The point was underscored a couple of months after its release when a novelty big band version was released to capitalise on the vogue for easy listening kitsch. The mid–1990s were big on irony and almost anything was acceptable as long as it came with sly quote marks to show it wasn't serious. Mike Flowers Pops illustrated the point with an orchestra whose version of 'Wonderwall' featured campy string arrangements and a pre-*Austin Powers* grin that seemed to sum up the mood of the time and, also reaching UK No 2, seemed for a long while to be the only song played on any given radio station other than the original version. It gave a surreal illustration of how much of a national institution the band were that they already had parodies as high profile as they were (within a year, Gallagher would give a jokey seal of approval to Oasis's own tribute act – No Way Sis).

Even a single featuring nothing more than an interview with the brothers managed to chart. 'Wibbling Rivalry' had been recorded the previous year as a straight conversation with journalist John Harris for the *NME*. The interview, which had been given not long after the band had aborted their Amsterdam gig, seemed to feature Noel more as the sensible older brother facing Liam's impish goading, yet both seemingly revelled in the very real entertainment value of their sparring. It only confirmed the public image of the brothers but with interest in all things Gallagher at fever pitch in 1995, the full conversation was put out by Fierce Panda, a small record label Harris ran with fellow writers Simon Williams and Paul Moody. 'Noel was great about it,' said Williams of the release and the single reached UK No 52, unprecedented for an interview.

Gallagher was the biggest thing in music for years and gave every sign of enjoying all of it immensely. Yet something had to give with the constant touring, promoting and press controversy and it was the song writing which suffered. For the first time he found he wasn't coming up with new songs. Focused on capitalising on his achievements, he didn't put down another tune for six to eight months after the album came out. But he talked about how he knew he already had a back catalogue to be proud of and if he had any doubts about what would come next, he kept them well hidden. 'The trick is, when songs aren't coming, then don't do anything,' he said. 'I imagine people write for the sake of it and that's why groups make shit albums. And we're lucky in that if we don't want to work we don't have to.'

By November, the band had taken in Europe, Japan and America and Gallagher now had his eye on London's Earls Court. It was a shed of a venue, but it was a very big one and it had played host to some of the biggest acts ever, a favourite destination for the monsters of the 1970s, including Pink Floyd with the full *Dark Side of the Moon* experience back in 1973. In early November, Oasis looked quite at home occupying the same space. Gallagher wielded a Union Jack guitar emblazoned with a Union Jack – a Sheraton customised for him by Epiphone (and commercially released as the Supernova – also available in Manchester City sky blue). It was superbly judged and looked totally right – all they needed was for Liam to have a customised Union Jack tambourine, which would have surely sold in vast amounts.

Oasis had immediately sold out a night at the 19,000 capacity venue on 4 November and had to add another date which also sold out. The shows attracted celebrities such as George Michael and Sting and, in a broad wink to Gallagher's oft-quoted influences, another tribute act – the Bootleg Beatles – were support. Oasis sounded great and looked in top shape on stage, every inch the world-beating rock stars but, while the money was rolling in, Gallagher was quoted as saying that everything went back into putting the shows on. 'There are no profits,' he said. Tracks from the two triumphant appearances were later issued on video as ... *There and Then*. Guigsy was absent due to exhaustion and was temporarily replaced by Scott McLeod.

By now Gallagher and Meg Mathews had moved up the hill from the din of Camden with its pop tourists hoping to catch a glimpse of rock stars in the Good Mixer to the rarefied environs of Belsize Park. There they bought a house which was soon christened Supernova Heights. Now Gallagher was just on the borders of Hampstead, the traditional home of the super-successful who liked to think of themselves as bohemian. Gallagher's place made no pretence at discretion, the name emblazoned above the door and he was under no illusions as to the impression he gave. Almost all of the band would end up living in the capital – 'We've got a little Mancunian corner of north London,' he said. 'You'll have noticed it – it's the area with no hubcaps on the cars.'

His new home became not only a magnet for star-studded parties, but a permanent hangout for paparazzi when they weren't following Liam around. Noel was seemingly unperturbed by the harassment, for the most part. 'I can take them all standing outside my house,' he later said of the press's appetite for Gallagher destruction. 'It's when they go knocking on my mam's door, because she's, like, 56. She doesn't know what's going on.'

Supernova Heights was a very physical symbol of his achievements and it was somewhere he considered to be safe. He could indulge every whim here and the place would be kitted out with everything including a jacuzzi with a mosaic of the Union Jack distorted under the water. Well-heeled locals were not used to the late night antics of the new arrivals but for years they would be a regular feature of the area.

The trappings of rock star success also included an 1967 Mark 2 Jaguar, straight out of *Inspector Morse*, with all the trimmings and modifications at £110,000. By the time it was kitted out and left in the garage, Gallagher – barely at home long enough to unpack his suitcase between tours – forgot it was at the garage. In any case, he couldn't drive.

CHAPTER 6

THIS IS HISTORY

'NOEL AND MARCUS [RUSSELL] CAME DOWN IN MARCH
AND DROVE THE ROLLER AROUND THE FIELD AND DOWN TO
THE BOTTOM OF THE HILL. NOEL JUST GOT OUT, HAD A
LOOK AROUND AND SAID, "RIGHT, WE'LL HAVE THIS."'
KNEBWORTH CONCERT PROMOTER, AUGUST 1996

Most of Oasis took to the stage at the understated but prestigious Royal Festival Hall in London for the recording of their *MTV Unplugged* session on 23 August 1996. Sitting down as the applause died away, Gallagher opened with a terse announcement. 'Good evening. Er, Liam ain't going to be with us tonight because he's got a sore throat. So you're stuck with the ugly four, as they say.'

Oasis erupted into a rare acoustic 'Hello' in which the Glitter chorus at last seemed to make sense. And Liam, though he was very much in the building and even made a brief appearance on stage, took no vocal duties. While it was far from the first time that Noel had taken over, he had never had to do so at such a high profile engagement and with the band's every movement by that point in 1996 being tracked by the media.

Commentators had been particularly keen to see how Oasis would handle *Unplugged*. The MTV show had become an institution which guaranteed a boost in musical credibility for anyone who took part. Few of those who took part could have needed to prove their ability to play without their guitar being plugged in, but the show spawned CD releases and notable reunions. One of its most notable successes, Robert Plant and Jimmy Page, nodded towards the conceit by calling their Led Zeppelin-inspired effort *Unledded*. Artists generally conjured an oversized acoustic guitar with a really good polish and added a string section to hint at classical sophistication. But if nothing else, *Unplugged* was a riposte to the over-production which had characterised such a chunk of '80s music and the strand that began in 1989 conferred seriousness on its participants.

On Oasis's big day not only did Noel Gallagher have to step into the spotlight, but the new line-up wasn't confirmed until shortly before the band were to take the stage. The record company cited laryngitis as the cause of Liam's no-show and the remaining band were augmented by the inevitable strings, brass, keyboardist Mike Rowe and another session regular, Mark Feltham blowing an impressive harmonica. That the performance went off faultlessly might well have been a cause for thought for

Liam, watching from a box with Patsy Kensit next to another filled with the band's friends. Noel looked up at one point in recognition: 'Oh, there you are.'

Yet MTV hesitated about broadcasting a front man-free Oasis, that slightly conservative stance they always took that seemed so at odds for a company dedicated to the broadcast of rock'n'roll in all its forms. It wasn't until later, following yet another media storm around Noel himself walking off an American tour later in the year amid speculation that the band would split up that they announced the airing. UK fans had to wait until 4 November to see the results on MTV, after its US debut. Yet despite a showing on terrestrial TV the following year, the show was never given a commercial release.

That the band were in some disarray by August was hardly a surprise. They'd played almost 40 shows already across the world, including the three biggest shows ever played in the UK and a triumphant return to their roots in Manchester. There were indications of how things might have gone differently. In May 1996, Noel holidayed in the exclusive island of Mustique in the West Indies. He spent a couple of weeks writing and then called out Owen Morris to demo with just an eight-track recorder, a drum machine and keyboard for string sounds. 'It's the first time I've ever done any demos,' he told *Select* that summer, 'But it sounds good.' Morris was hoping to get a couple of songs down, but Gallagher's writing lay-off after …*Morning Glory* didn't seem to have done him any harm.

'The first night he reeled off 15 songs on the acoustic,' said Morris. 'Then we piled through them in a week, midday to 7pm in this chalet by the airport.' It was here that the airplane sounds which opened the album were recorded. 'It's easy with Noel because you make decisions on the hoof – chop that... stick that in, bung it down. Guitar overdubs and backing vocals as well. The Mustique tape's amazing, really cool, although it sounds shit because of the drum box ... The words, most of the arrangements and the running order were sorted on Mustique too. He's got big balls that man. He did that week's work and that was it.' It wasn't the entire album – 'Magic Pie' came later and a number of its songs were dropped. But in the main these were sun-kissed sessions, when everything flowed, back to basics and fuelled by run and smoke. 'The Mustique session was the last good recording I did with Noel. The arrangements were shorter than on the album,' Morris told Keith Cameron for Q some years later. 'Noel was performing well and the vibe was positive.'

In Mustique Gallagher got together again with Johnny Depp who was on holiday with girlfriend Kate Moss. Having been part of the War Child album with Noel, Depp, who had his own band, had also contributed to sound-tracks and been a guest player with artists such as Shane MacGowan. This sort of casual celebrity holiday hangout was normal for Gallagher now, though he was always self-aware enough in interviews to flag up his new circle of friends. Meg Mathews and Kate Moss were already friends and Gallagher went to visit Depp while he was staying at Mick Jagger's house on the island. 'Meg and Kate are in the back getting pissed,' he later said, 'Johnny's in this little adjoining room writing a script for this film, I'm sat in Mick Jagger's fucking front room with an acoustic guitar writing a song for the new album, looking around at all these original Andy Warhol paintings, going, "Fucking hell..."'

It was a toy piano belonging to one of Jagger's children which was recorded and wonkily introduced the track 'Be Here Now'. 'The opening's played on that, slowed down,' said Gallagher. 'I was pressing that one key for about two hours, Meg going, "Will you fucking shut up!" Anyway, I nicked it – me from Burnage. I can't help it. Mick can have it back if he wants.' When it later came to recording the album itself, Owen Morris said one of the greatest intros of all time was 'Honky Tonk Women'. They discovered it shared the same key as the toy piano and Gallagher was away.

It was those kind of little sparks of inspiration that flew in Mustique. 'The first part of "Fade In/Fade Out" was recorded in a little fucking shack on the beach,' said Gallagher. 'We were drunk one night and I borrowed his [Depp's] slide guitar and tried to play this solo and it was absolutely dreadful. So he sat down and played it and got it in one take ... He doesn't actually think he's any good, but he's a fine guitarist ... [when] we were rehearsing for the tour, it took me about six months to work out what he was actually playing.'

There was something playful and unpressurised in the way that Gallagher and Owen Morris described their time in Mustique. It was incomprehensibly far from the roots which had inspired *Definitely Maybe*, but Gallagher could hardly pretend to be there now. There was little of that kind of relaxation to be found elsewhere in the year, which was characterised by hard playing and hard partying. And it was that lifestyle which would be reflected in *Be Here Now*.

The year had begun in fine style with 'Don't Look Back in Anger' released on 19 February to become the second UK No 1 for the band as ...*Morning Glory* continued to sell in vast quantities. Even non-fans of the band were relieved to hear anything that displaced 'Spaceman' by Babylon Zoo, the jeans-advertising one-hit wonders whose gimmick of sounding speeded up and then going all slow and slightly Bowie-like had inexplicably done very well. Following 'Spaceman', there were more corporate music industry larks on the day of the release of 'Look Back in Anger' with the Brit Awards.

The annual ceremony was still a byword for the most conservative aspects of rock and pop. Phil Collins and Annie Lennox may not have won something every year, but even though Oasis amassed nominations across the board, it certainly felt like they did. Even with Chris Evans staying up later than his Radio 1 breakfast show should have allowed him in order to host the awards, it was still a night not expected to be full of surprises. And then Pulp's Jarvis Cocker disrupted Michael Jackson's messiah complex 'Earth

Song' with a splendidly disrespectful wiggle of his fashionably skinny Brit Pop posterior. He attracted huge amounts of censure in the press until they realised that he hadn't shown his actual bottom and that, anyway, everyone was on Cocker's side and after that all fire was turned on Jackson's jaw-dropping welcoming of the children of the world unto his arms. Chris Evans... Jarvis Cocker... suddenly it seemed like the new generation were finally taking over and they were showing that they were clever with it.

But, yes, there were still a lot of the old guard on hand. Gallagher laid into them, genuinely furious that fans should be so short-changed. 'What about Björk and PJ Harvey? Annie Lennox? What's she done in her entire fucking life, ever, ever, ever? It's a fucking scandal, man. We'll come here, we'll get pissed and we'll take the awards. But I tell you what, they're presented by fucking idiots.' Oasis made off with awards for Best Group, and Best Album. When they were presented with the Best Video award by Michael Hutchence of soul rockers INXS, Gallagher commented almost as an afterthought, 'Has-beens shouldn't present fucking awards to gonnabes.' It was hard to disagree, though by 2007 it would be Oasis who were the establishment and up for the eminently respectable Outstanding Contribution to Music award.

Maine Road stadium was the home of Gallagher's beloved Manchester City. It stood in the Moss Side district of the city and the club was based there from 1923 until their move east in 2003 to the new City of Manchester stadium. There had been plans for other sporting uses for the old site, but the following year Maine Road was demolished to make way for residential properties. As fellow Man City fan and Bolton-born broadcaster of early Oasis numbers Mark Radcliffe said, 'Maine Road was one of the last grounds connected ... closely to working class housing.'

For those very personal and emotional reasons, a gig at Maine Road was a homecoming for Gallagher in every sense. And there were two – on 27 and 28 April after one night sold out just as fast as the Earls Court show had the previous year. Out came the Union Jack Supernova with the band augmented by musicians including a string section. Songs from the sets also made it to the ... *There and Then* video and DVD release. It was a triumph with even the b-sides received as if they were No 1s. There was even the traditional inter-brother grumble to liven things up further. On the second night the Gallaghers had a few words in the middle of 'Whatever' and while his younger brother stalked off to one side, Noel took over the vocals. But by their standards even this was rather good natured and while Liam rattled his tambourine, soaking up the atmosphere on stage with an oversized, handrolled cigarette, an entirely unrattled Noel finished the song, segueing into the Beatles' 'Octopus's Garden'. The customary encores of 'I Am the Walrus' and b-side cover 'Cum on Feel the Noize' completed the victory parade.

Following the first gig, Gallagher spoke of how he was

overwhelmed by thoughts of when he used to come to the ground as a kid and of one of his team's finest goalies. 'I used to come every Saturday, watch big Joe Corrigan and all the rest of it and now it's us. It's like, "Yes, thank you..." Just need to take some time to think – I'm all over the place. After Sunday [28th, second gig] it's gonna be three months off. Got to be. I'm still mad for it, we all are, but I gotta have some time out.'

It seemed as if it wasn't possible to top the emotion of Maine Road, but Gallagher always planned to go bigger. On 7 May the next move in the master plan was unveiled first thing in the morning on Chris Evans' breakfast show. On 10 and 11 August, they would play in the grounds of Knebworth House in the Hertfordshire countryside just north of London. The demand was phenomenal. Even though 250,000 tickets were made available in total, it wasn't anywhere near enough. More than 2.5 million people scrambled to attempt securing their place in what was effectively more of a mini-festival than a regular gig. Gallagher ended that momentous May with the news that he was to be given an Ivor Novello award for song writing – but as it was to be shared with Blur he turned it down.

The gigs that summer were to take place while the country was already in an exuberant mood. Football – never closer to music as a form of release than then – was coming home. This was taken to be true not least because comedians Frank Skinner and David Baddiel bellowed it in 'Three Lions', the official song they put out with the Lightning Seeds' Ian Broudie. Adding to the atmosphere of general anticipation were Tony Blair and New Labour, waiting in the wings as the Conservatives failed to capitalise on an economic boom and burgeoning sense of prosperity. The country was waking up and wanting to party, but they didn't want to do it with Prime Minister John Major. Both pop and football had gained a new mass respectability and despite England's inevitable defeat on penalties to Germany, there was no Glastonbury Festival that year, leaving room for a big musical event that Oasis were intent on filling.

There was no doubt that they could do it. Even when Gallagher wasn't in the room, his influence was already being felt in a younger wave of bands. Ocean Colour Scene were one of the support acts at Knebworth and anyone in such proximity to Gallagher could be included in what the *NME* called 'Noelrock', even though they had been around for a number of years. But Gallagher had helped Ocean Colour Scene to secure wider prominence, though by contrast with the garrulous Gallagher, they had a reputation for shunning the press and for being far more earnest. Yet they hadn't just been plucked at random by Gallagher as the 'Noelrock' epithet might suggest – the two acts went back a number of years. Guitarist Steve Cradock, who also played with Paul Weller, told *Select*, 'Noel used to come and see us whenever we played the Plash Club in London and we saw Oasis play at our local pub, the Jug of Ale, in

February 1994.' But they realised that Gallagher had kicked down a lot of doors and, although they had been going seven years, their 1992 eponymous album wasn't as important as the 1996 follow-up. 'To us *Moseley Shoals* is our debut album. We definitely feel like that. We even refer to it as our first album.'

This was music that parents as well as their kids could like – it was familiar. But as Gallagher himself pointed out, there was more to their success than just leafing through the classic rock songbook to find the good bits. 'People think I just sit there and listen to Mott the Hoople b-sides and then write a song,' he said. 'It ain't like that.' He was always more open to other ways of doing things than he let on – as his collaboration with the Chemical Brothers would show later that year – and he had an instinct for the commercial which required less of an ego than he was often credited with and more of an innate ability to think like the typical music fan he was.

Gallagher had created his own niche with Oasis and it was more that the media were keen to find other acts to put in orbit around them. But when any band who had some kind of northern grit to them and a way with a lofty chorus were included in the pigeonhole, it soon became redundant and arguably later a drag on the career of bands like Embrace. It was hardly their fault that they had brothers as singer and guitarist in the shape of Danny and Richard McNamara. They might benefit from a boost in the press to begin with but it would be hard to cut the

Gallagher parka-strings. All bands had to fight to establish their own identity and Gallagher had been very savvy in repeatedly pointing out where his own portrait should go in the rock wall of fame, but there was something particularly deadening about the hand of Oasis on an act's shoulder. For groups like Hurricane #1 it was more like the regular descriptions of new singer-songwriters as the new Bob Dylan. Such was the charisma and weight of expectation for defining a generation that they couldn't help but suffer by comparison. But if nothing else, Gallagher was showing that he was powerful enough to carry off the gigs in Knebworth.

They had kicked off the big gigs at Balloch Castle park near Loch Lomond, Scotland on 3 and 4 August. The Oasis hysteria was in full effect at the far north of the UK with support including Manic Street Preachers and Black Grape. As the audience waited impatiently in the break before the main act came on, the sky was dark with the bottles being thrown at the stage. Forthcoming *Be Here Now* tracks such as 'My Big Mouth' and 'It's Getting Better (Man!!)' were enthusiastically received – but then, everything was. Some 40,000 fans saw the band each night, but this was little more than a warm-up for what was to come in Knebworth.

Knebworth was on a scale which hadn't been seen since the glory days of the Rolling Stones and Led Zeppelin. Punk had made it completely unfashionable to host such debauched extravaganzas, but more practically the sound technology had also been so basic that the practice had died out partly through dire quality. But with music now having so much more history it was possible to reach back from the 1990s and combine the scale of the events from the 1970s with the passion of the punks to make the case that Oasis were doing it on a grandiose scale but somehow still keeping it real. Gallagher and the rest wore definitively non-rock star clothes, they looked like part of the audience who supported them. This wasn't the hammer of the Gods come to grace their fans – this was an enormous event cast as a shared experience.

The indie image was unshakeable. Behind Oasis were still Creation, who had done deals with major labels and were financially secure and yet were perceived as being staunchly individualist. Having had bands such as Ride and Primal Scream and a rock'n'roll boss in the shape of Alan McGee, they were creative and as enthusiastic as ever about music, no matter how much things were changing with Oasis. And then there was the press coverage, with the gigs that August being covered everywhere from the music weeklies through the monthlies to the tabloid and broadsheet nationals. The red-tops focused inevitably on the celebrity side of things and the Scottish press tried to drum up some scare stories of how devastating the influx of Oasis fans could be to Loch Lomond, but essentially the story was reported positively. The statistics were mind-boggling and yet it almost seemed as if these were indie bar gigs, albeit ones on a huge scale. Like all successful emperors, Gallagher had made his invading forces appealing enough so that everyone felt, if they wanted, they could take something from Oasis without compromising themselves.

Not only Oasis but the rise of the summer festival season in the 1990s would bring these kind of gigantic celebrations of music, chemical toilets included, back into the frontline of entertainment. You might have to queue for hours for those toilets and for drinks and for getting back home afterwards, but you could say you were there and your ears would ring for days afterwards as a souvenir. It seemed as if everyone had turned up. The VIP area was massive and the guest list, according to journalist John Harris, ran to some 7,000 names from all areas of the media. Some in the music press were calling the shows not just the biggest but the best of all time and special editions of music magazines were issued to celebrate the weekend.

But maybe it was possible to be too big. This was what was beginning to bother some people, Alan McGee among them. He thought it was too big for Creation – too big for Oasis, he said. The PA system was one of the loudest ever heard, the screens to rely the action to those at the back were huge and the acts playing alongside were hardly anything as lowly as support – among them Manic Street Preachers, the Prodigy, the Chemical Brothers, Dreadzone, the Charlatans represented a cross-section of the biggest and most interesting bands around. The Bootleg Beatles were also there.

Manics' bassist Nicky Wire said, 'I'm not sure Oasis

realised the gigantic nature of what they were doing. The moment for me was when John Squire came on and played "Champagne Supernova".'

Although he had never really suffered from nerves, the sheer scale of the gig concentrated Gallagher's mind but he was more laidback by the second night. The brothers enjoyed much more between song banter than before. When Noel said, 'This is history. You're making history,' to the crowd and repeated himself, his brother replied, 'This is Knebworth! What are you on about?'

John Squire made his appearance having only just left the Stone Roses that March. His character was sketched out by Gallagher in typically sharp fashion. 'You can have 15 minutes' conversation with John Squire over about five hours: "How are you doing, John?" "Yeah... I'm..." "I'll just put the kettle on while you think that one over, eh, John?"' But Gallagher could still be overawed by meeting his heroes. He was oblivious to the gigantic crowd and the firestorm of lighters that were raised towards him when John Squire started playing. 'Check him out, what he's doing!' he later said he was thinking. 'That's another moment in my life. He's never played with anyone else bar the Stone Roses and we've never played with anyone else bar us lot.' But for the most part, Gallagher later said of Knebworth, 'We were too busy doing it to worry about it. If we'd thought about it, well, I'd have certainly worn a better outfit. And gone to bed a little bit earlier. And tried to keep Liam off the sauce ...

'I remember us just being sort of normal. We were worried about other stuff... "Have you got the beers backstage? Are they cold? And have you got Sky?" Stuff like that.'

Asked – as he was more than once – whether Oasis were bigger than God, Gallagher had a readier reply than usual in the years after those two gigs. 'I would hope we mean more to people than putting money in a church basket and saying ten "Hail Marys" on a Sunday. Has God played Knebworth recently?' But even God took at least one day off. The band might have taken a few months rest between Maine Road and Knebworth, but more than ever they would have benefitted now from time to think about what to do next. Even Gallagher seemed not to know what there was left for him to achieve. 'Nothing,' he said in the immediate aftermath of Knebworth. I'd like to do a big free gig somewhere. I know it sounds corny, but a big gig for charity, just to give something back. It's like, we've made enough money out of this now.'

It seemed as if even Gallagher himself wasn't sure of his emotions after the shows. 'I can safely say we won't be going any fucking bigger than this, because to be quite honest, we can't supply the demand for the band at the moment. We're trying, but to do things like this, it's just a fucking pain in the arse. It's brilliant to do it, but I wouldn't fancy doing it again,' he said in an interview with *Select* shortly before the second night. 'What do you do? All you can do is sit and laugh at it. We're laughing our heads off. We don't know what to do anymore. Where do you go? Sooner or later it's going to get like that in America. It's just mental. You can't ask for advice off anyone who's been there before, because no one has. Apart from fucking Dave Gilmour and that. You know, I've got a few things to say to Phil Collins, but asking for advice would be fucking one of them.' This was, he seemed to be realising, as big as anyone could get – and yet still there was no sign that they were letting up in pace. 'No, fuck that. We like doing it too much. We'd love to go back and do smaller gigs, but then, a small gig now is like Earls Court ... As long as the ball keeps rolling... who knows?' The answer was *Be Here Now*, but what was uppermost in his mind was interesting. 'We're not splitting up and I've got no plans to go solo in the next five years. I suppose a solo record is inevitable. We are gonna have to do other things.'

First there was that infamous MTV performance which they got through less than two weeks later and then just three days later they were off again to the US. It was to be a strenuous three weeks. Not least because they got no further than Heathrow when Liam said because he was having difficulties finding a new home, he was going to have to sort it out there and then. 'I said, "Right, see you in a bit",' Noel remembered, 'fully expecting him to come back in five minutes' time. And he didn't.' The plan had been to sort out all the personal stuff in the break they took after the Maine Road gigs – but Liam needed longer. For his part, he was said to have been told that his house in north London's St John's Wood, a couple of miles away from Supernova Heights, had been sold and he needed to get out by the end of the week. For Noel, it was all about how they should be letting the fans down in the USA, but he laughed the incident off in the press as just another day for Oasis. Years later he even commented, 'Admittedly, he did buy a nice house.'

Liam made it clear that he wasn't anyway well enough to sing and had only ever planned to travel with the band until he was given the medical all-clear. One way or another, it seemed, Noel was going to have to keep on vocal duties for longer. But now the band was heading off to the US without its singer. 'I can sing as well as Liam can,' Gallagher said, 'but I am no front man and it's going to be hard work. The show must go on, which is a motto at the moment. If he telephones, I am telling him I expect him to be in the band when we get back, but you never know with Liam.'

On other occasions, Noel had talked about how the band would deliberately wind his brother up to get him energised. It had some beneficial effects on him in the studio, bringing out his rawest performances. 'The more you call him a cunt, the more you bring the papers in and say, "Look what they're saying about you, you soft bastard!", he'll just go in there and deliver straight away.' But this was very different and Noel was anyway aware of how much strain being the front man put Liam under and even as he was making fun of him, it was clear he was concerned. 'To be honest, I would've thought he'd have gone under by now ... but he's hung in there.'

In the event, Gallagher only took the first date at the Rosemont Horizon arena in Illinois, the band supported by Manic Street Preachers and Screaming Trees. The venue was about two thirds full, Gallagher having given fans the option of having their money back. Oasis played their usual set, but for the first time Gallagher took vocals for big hits such as 'Roll With It' as well as the likes of 'Cigarettes & Alcohol', which he had performed alone before, alongside much loved b-sides such as 'Acquiesce'. Some objects were thrown at the stage and there were a few disgruntled boos but Noel never faltered. He made the briefest of references to the absence. 'You've probably heard my brother's not here this evening,' he said. But although one reporter noted that someone shouted back, 'Where's your fucking brother?', the fans for the most part seemed to enjoy the show immensely.

By the time the band got to the next date, the Palace in Michigan, Liam had returned. But by then his brother had shown he could carry the band himself. It was far from the first time that he had taken over vocals, even in the US and he had his usual acoustic set – which he played as normal at Rosemont. Yet there was something about having carried off a prestigious TV performance like MTV and shouldered an arena gig from the start in short succession which under-lined his fundamental belief that as much as he might argue with his brother or enjoy the rock star lifestyle, Gallagher wasn't going to allow the empire he had built to simply collapse. And yet, while he was as calm, understated and assured as he had been on MTV, he nevertheless took up his usual position stage left at Rosemont, as if to underline that there was a still a vacancy at the centre.

'Some might say that Noel Gallagher is Oasis,' said the *Chicago Sun-Times*. 'They wouldn't be too far off. Sure, some fans missed vocalist Liam Gallagher ... But the wild ovations they awarded his brother ... showed that the songs were more important than the singer.'

Not that the constant touring was that much easier for Noel. The vast distances of the North American continent were a test for any band and they were playing audiences smaller than they were used to seeing in the UK and each audience, night after night, expected to see exactly what their British equivalents had been used to for the past few months. Gallagher was also aware that when he came off tour they were due to go back into the studio and he would have to work out new material and then the whole thing was due to start again. With the volatile relationship between the brothers at the centre of the band it seemed unlikely they would last until 1999, let alone 2009. They were as bigger a draw as any band in the world at that point and they were selling millions of records in the US, but they still had a long way to go. 'Oasis was an unknown to most Americans just a year ago.

In Britain, Oasis isn't just any band, but *the* band,' said one US journalist. 'The Top 10 hit "Wonderwall" hasn't catapulted Oasis to that sort of stature yet in this country, but I wouldn't bet against them. They're patient, talented and unpredictable.'

Gallagher would never see his band become the kind of global brand in the manner of a U2 or a Coldplay – and although for a while that prospect seemed tantalisingly close, in a way it probably didn't suit characters so totally identified with the UK. And despite the tough reputation around the band, it was that level of ubiquity which Gallagher was ambitious for. 'U2, man,' he told *Hot Press*. 'Totally. I've said that to people and they go, "Ugggh, fucking hell! U2." Yeah... think about it. For them four to stay together that long, with the same management and people around them, is fucking staggering. America didn't break them – they broke America ... and when you meet them they're the nicest fucking guys in the world.'

Oasis had done better than the Brit Pop bands they came up with, but it still wasn't enough. 'Americans just fundamentally do not get it,' said Gallagher on another occasion. 'That is the one thing about Yanks. They. Do. No. Get. It.' There had been more excitement from the USA while Oasis were the hot new things and for a while they sold better over in the States than at home. But while the more eccentric antics which came along with Oasis played well in the UK, it became badly lost in translation.

'They were nice people,' said Gallagher of the US label, 'but they could not understand our band who were, at the time, the biggest band in the world. We treated it with contempt, really.'

Oasis were being propelled around the continent as if they were out there for the first time. Nothing to prove back home and yet here were these gigs that might have been many times larger than anything Gallagher could have done with Inspiral Carpets but were still very much the kind of slog Oasis had long left behind in the UK. Everyone in the band was complaining and yet it was Gallagher himself who needed a break more than most. Getting other people from the record company involved to sort out logistics hadn't helped much in terms of taking a load from him. Things had long been too big for him to carry them personally, but there was always another date to do. He was alarmed to find that tours were being booked and plans were being drawn up that he had to fit around, rather than the other way around. He had a huge appetite for working hard for Oasis but events constantly seemed to be sliding out of his control.

Everyone dealt with the daily realities of life as a part of Oasis in their own way. During the MTV awards of 4 September in the US, Liam was again in full throttle on stage, swearing and singing about a 'Champagne supernova up yer bum'. When it was reported from North Carolina that, for the second time in the band's US career, Gallagher himself was coming home early on 11 September, it seemed partly inevitable but also all the press needed to report that the band were splitting up.

Oasis had just played near Washington and had flown south to play Charlotte in North Carolina when there was another altercation. Gigs had been cancelled before, but this was played out in front of the cameras. Without a specific denial from the band that they were splitting up, blanket coverage followed as the brothers came home early, Noel alone and Liam, not for the last time, with the rest of the band. They were still expected in Atlanta on Friday the 13th and at three other gigs, as the balance of the US leg of the tour was cancelled.

There hadn't been a great number of dates to drop but that wasn't the point as a sizeable question mark appeared over the band in the US. Despite their great success and talent, did they really have the drive to fulfil their ambition? Gallagher's work ethic and determination to realise their potential could only stretch so far and the fallout certainly didn't help the band's chances of conquering the US. At least, while the music press speculated and the tabloids swooped on anyone who'd ever met a member of the band, the creative pressure was off Gallagher. There was at last the luxury of time to think about what to do – whether to record and not tour or to press on as normal. They had concertinaed the promoting of a massively successful album into little over a year. Gallagher had played the same songs night after night as if every date might be his last. He needed to get a little distance from his work.

A spokesman for Oasis said, 'This so-called crisis has been blown out of all proportion. The band are still very much a band. It was funny to watch the media writing the band's obituary one day and having to backtrack frantically the next.' The *Sun* in particular had done one of its favourite tricks in carpet-bombing reports of the band's sensational splits before then saying it was the wave of protest which prompted Gallagher to re-form the band. The full-blown Oasis phenomenon was something that nobody fully controlled. In the meantime, the rest of the tour, with dates all over the world, was cancelled. Nothing was being ruled out – Gallagher was even talking with the rest of the band about becoming a studio-only outfit.

There were financial implications in terms of compensation for the rest of the tour and the engagements already missed, but perhaps an extended break was worth it. By the time they got back in the studio and Gallagher soon remembered how much he loved the life. 'I think that as soon as we started making the record we just said, "What are we moaning about? It's a fucking top laugh."' There was one final date in December in Minnesota before the hundred plus-date ...Morning Glory tour finally juddered to a halt, leaving Oasis battered but now, if not the biggest, undoubtedly the hottest and one of the biggest bands on the planet.

Gallagher hadn't even taken that much time off, though he got to see the fruits of a collaboration with the Chemical Brothers become a smash hit. It had been recorded long before, but it was a weird answer to the question of what the world might sound like after Oasis. Perhaps something of a precursor to his collaborations with Amorphous Androgynous, 'Setting Sun' was as blistering a number as anything Oasis had done. Gallagher had known the Chemical Brothers for a while and they were a couple he could safely introduce to even the most traditionalist of Oasis fan. The Chemicals were, along with the Prodigy, the dance act it was okay for rock'n'roll fans to like, as Oasis fans had demonstrated at Knebworth. But of the two UK No 1 singles taken from *Dig Your Own Hole*, the album itself coming out the following year, September's 'Setting Sun' was the more expansive and soaring. The insistent 'Block Rockin' Beats' seemed to be everywhere, but it was Gallagher's contribution which was the more unusual and the biggest hint to date that he wasn't only the six-string wonder of legend.

The new sound of Oasis was not to follow such a dramatic departure. The band began work the month after the US tour, in October, at Abbey Road, but it was hard to concentrate with the constant circus around the band. If it wasn't the drugs, hangers on and the party-goers, it was the sight of a tabloid journalist lurking around every corner in the building itself. The Beatles' home ground could have been a natural fit for Gallagher and engineer

Nick Brine remembered that, 'the atmosphere started off great. It always was amongst the band and crew during these sessions at Abbey Road. It just didn't suit the band at that point though, and this soon changed the vibe.' In the end, they decided it would be better to relocate, though not before they had played back all the Beatles albums at top volume and as Brine remembered: 'Got everyone buzzing.'

Oasis wouldn't return to Abbey Road until *Dig Out Your Soul* in 2008. In early November the band pitched up not far from London, in the peaceful surroundings of the Surrey countryside in Ridge Farm studios, staying on site. And although there was still a lot of distraction around, there were also compensations in being out there. 'It was like being the band again,' Gallagher recalled. 'Just sitting up all night talking bullshit and making music.'

The focus of Oasis was being lost in the crazy life that attended their success. And yet Gallagher never lost sight of making music. It just got a little hazy at times. 'It wasn't like a seedy situation,' he later said. 'We were at work. We weren't passed out on the floor with a bottle of Jack Daniel's. We were partying while we were working.'

Yet there was no focus, objectivity or restraint. Creation wasn't the corporate kind of label to start laying down the law and demanding to know what the lead single would be. Which was good when everything was running smoothly, but if Gallagher was not only the main creative powerhouse but also guiding the production to a great extent, there really wasn't anyone around with sufficient authority to question the direction of the sessions. Nobody was listening. They were all making music, partying and nobody, at that time, was going to tell the man behind the biggest noise on the planet to slow down.

CHAPTER 7

AROUND THE WORLD

'JUST IMAGINE IF THAT ALBUM HAD SOLD 30 MILLION COPIES.
I PROBABLY WOULD HAVE GROWN A MOUSTACHE
AND STARTED WEARING A FUCKING CAPE.'
NOEL GALLAGHER ON *BE HERE NOW*

There were those who voted in the May 1997 general election who not only hadn't been old enough to vote last time there had been a Labour government, but hadn't even been born. With John Major wiped out, 18 years of Conservative rule juddered to a halt. Three months later, at the end of July, Prime Minister Tony Blair hosted a reception at No 10 with guests including Noel Gallagher.

Blair's premiership would be remembered for other things, as it turned out, but in those first few days the showbiz fraternity in Downing Street loomed large. Gallagher would long be reminded of that picture of him greeting the country's new leader, champagne glass in hand

(Gallagher) and toothy grin in place (Blair). Alan McGee was captured staring enigmatically from somewhere behind his left shoulder. It was a defining image. Although some in the press said that this was rock'n'roll being accepted and tamed in some way by the establishment, it was hardly as if Gallagher had set out to be a subversive fringe element. Playing the uplifting anthems of Oasis to hundreds of thousands of people over August the previous year did not qualify as an attempt at rebellion.

Gallagher had anyway been far from the only one to be enthused by the sensation of change in the country. With the Tories out of the way it felt very much as if a dead hand had been taken off the controls of the UK. It was true, though, that other Brit Pop stars stayed away, Damon Albarn quoted as saying, 'Enjoy the schmooze, comrade.' Yet if things couldn't only get better in the way it had been suggested they would, no politician could possibly have lived up to the expectations placed largely personally on Tony Blair as a young, bright man of the people. And even the hardest of cynics would have been hard-pressed to predict the calamity on his reputation inflicted by the war in Iraq, particularly given how successful Blair would be in leading the Northern Ireland peace process and on intervening in the Balkans and the Kosovo conflict. If the photograph of Blair and Gallagher remained potent, it was perhaps because there was a sense with both the young men captured in that photograph that they very quickly in their very different careers achieved the positions they wanted –

and, despite having total confidence in their own abilities, were on some level not entirely sure what to do with what they'd won.

But both were also ruthlessly pragmatic and deeply populist, Gallagher later being just as up front in saying how he was among those who felt let down by Blair after 9/11 and the Iraq war. 'I tell you what New Labour have achieved. They've actually destroyed politics in this country. Because I don't know anyone who, next time around, is gonna fucking vote. It means nothing,' he said in 2006. At the time he was then speaking he had again got the mood of the country right, in the sense that a limp Conservative-Liberal coalition replaced Labour in the 2010 election. 'Left and right doesn't mean anything – it's all this middle ground that's just nothing ... Life's still shit for most people ... everyone can afford an iPod, so they think life's fucking great.'

But Gallagher was also clear about the limitations he felt in expressing political views as a musician. Talking about 'Up in the Sky' around the time of *Definitely Maybe*, Gallagher had already made it clear what he thought about making grand statements. 'This band is about the music, it's about the songs,' he said. 'We're overtly political once every five years, when we all go out and vote Labour. But then we go back to being a band again.' If he was political in his public life at all, it was only in as much as he was generally optimistic and wanted people to make a difference to their lives.

For Tony Blair's part, he had been in the audience at the Brit Awards in 1996 to hear Noel Gallagher say that there were 'seven people in this room tonight giving a little hope to young people in this country.' Gallagher named the five members of Oasis and Creation boss Alan McGee, who had been by their side as they received their award, and Tony Blair. When it came to his invite to the celebratory bash in 1997, there was no agenda. 'I didn't go thinking, "I endorse this government's policies in every respect." I went to have a look at the curtains.' That was the heart of it for him. Being asked to go to the Prime Minister's residence was simply a thrill. 'I'd only signed off the dole four years earlier,' Gallagher said, 'and I arrived at Downing Street in a Rolls Royce. I was laughing all the way there.' It was the chocolate-brown Rolls Royce that Gallagher had once told Alan McGee would be the crowning symbol of all the success he wanted. And now McGee was in a position just to buy it for him. By that time in the Oasis story, with their star at its highest, it seemed a totally sensible notion that the new Labour leader would want to entertain Noel Gallagher.

Later on, Gallagher would even say that he knew he would attract criticism for the encounter. He might have become caught up in the general high political spirits in a way which a less impetuous operator might have avoided, but his common touch hadn't deserted him in attending the Downing Street party. Just as he did with his lyrics, he had tapped into the general affection for new Labour in the country in the way that it played along with the country's yearning for something more compassionate in society. The Blair administration had inherited an enormous amount of goodwill and found a country more at ease with itself than ever before – ideology was out, to be replaced by a vague feeling that somehow we were all in this together, something regularly reflected in Gallagher's lyrics. In interview, Gallagher himself always came across as a liberal – small 'l' – anti-racist, pro-multiculturalism and inclusivity. As any of his songs attested he was only after a better standard of living and working hard to attain it. If it didn't happen he was all about blocking out reality in the most amusing way possible. This was all very New Labour.

In a more practical sense, the meeting between Blair and Gallagher came as Oasis was gearing up for the release of their third album. The media were frenziedly building the launch into a national drama and the Downing Street party simply came somewhere between another UK No 1 single in early July's 'D'You Know What I Mean?' and the launch of *Be Here Now* towards the end of August. No 10 was just another day for Noel Gallagher.

The album had been completed over the early part of the year, though between its sessions Gallagher had still found time to kick off another media storm at the *NME* Brat awards in January, when he commented that taking drugs was 'like getting up and having a cup of tea in the morning.' He was speaking up in defence of Brian Harvey, the former singer with East 17 who had been sacked by his band earlier in the month for apparently condoning drug taking, though he would later rejoin. The press coverage of Gallagher this time around was accompanied by criticism from MPs and he said, 'If saying a few seemingly outrageous things has helped to instigate an open and honest debate about drug abuse in this country, then I'm pleased ... I've never condoned the use of drugs. I slam as hypocrites those politicians who condemn drug abuse as criminal, thinking they are doing something positive.'

While ecstasy had been well-known as the drug of choice for clubbers for some years by now and the age of the rave was well into its middle years, it had been less than two years since the death of young Leah Betts on the drug had sparked a scare campaign, ably fanned by the *Mail* and the other usual suspects looking for manufactured outrage. But now perhaps things were changing a little bit as many in public life stepped forward to agree with Gallagher that some kind of reasoned debate was required. 'The best thing about that whole scenario,' Gallagher later said, 'was I've got a cover of the *Daily Mirror* that says "98 per cent back Noel on drugs". Which is great headline – one for the grandkids, innit?' One of his most interesting points – rather lost in the noise over yet another Gallagher soundbite – was to observe how any kind of press coverage could be turned to the advantage of all parties. In the aftermath of his comment he had been approached by people directly affected by the issues who suggested he might make amends by making a sizeable donation. Worthy organisations, he said, would start off 'with this big compassion and guilt thing and then at the end of the line it all boils down to "How much money are you going to give us?"' Both sides had their agendas.

The story had broken while Gallagher was in the north of the country and he had to cut short his trip to return to London and deal with the press fallout. He arrived to find he couldn't get into his own house due to the media scrum in the Belsize Park street. Land Rovers were parked everywhere with huge satellite dishes on their roofs. 'So I said to the geezer driving, "Go past our house because I've got to get a picture of that."

This was just another salvo in what seemed to be a continuous campaign to keep Oasis permanently in the tabloids and work on the new album continued uninterrupted. It was a very different record. If the first two releases had been about dreaming of the freedom implicit in rock'n'roll and then living it, part of what inspired the third one was what happened next. Something that Gallagher had briefly described as 'wishing I was still fucking back at home doing what I was doing before it all kicked off'. Such a throwaway comment might not have been the most positive place to start the creative process, but it was a reflection of how all consuming his world had become. He would later distance himself from the album, as would much of the press once the Oasis backlash got properly underway, but despite the excess around the making of *Be Here Now*, there was still a focus to what Gallagher did.

Engineer Nick Brine told the website oasis-recordinginfo.co.uk that the demos Gallagher had put together in Mustique guided the direction of the sessions even before the band left Abbey Road. They had, he said, such 'an attitude and feel that I could instantly get a feel for where they were going,' he said. 'They were stripped back compared to how the album ended up, but the attitude and intent was evident.' But those more straight-forward ideas would soon become difficult to pick out with each successive layer of guitar added during the recording process.

'I wish we'd let *(What's the Story) Morning Glory?* settle and go away,' Gallagher later told *Spin*. 'It was still No 5 in the Billboard 100 when we started making *Be Here Now*. I wish someone who's paid to be bright and clever had told us to go away and do a bit of living. But we were fuelled by youth and cocaine. Everything was going to be bigger and better. We were surrounded by people telling us it was the greatest thing they'd ever heard. When you're the cash cow ... people are always going to cheer you on, whatever.' Very little seemed to slow Gallagher down at the best of times. Even with all the rock'n'roll paraphernalia of drugs and partying, even when he'd seen through two of the most successful albums of recent times, he seemed incapable of taking it easy, enjoying his success and thinking through what was going to happen yet. It was as if he always had to be moving on, forever escaping the unstable background of his earliest days.

Other bands, even his pantomime least favourites Radiohead, were taking more of a step back to reassess where they were going. *OK Computer* had been a UK No 1 earlier in the summer with songs that built upon the promise of their previous efforts but when they finally returned in 2000 would be with something very different indeed with *Kid A*. Much though Gallagher seemed to enjoy teasing Radiohead in interview about their supposed pretensions, he also appeared to be genuinely intrigued if ambivalent about the prospects of doing something completely other with music. Even when he eventually went solo, he would have both the more traditional High Flying Birds alongside the Amorphous Androgynous route, as if still not sure which way to jump.

Music itself had generally always flowed quite easily through him, yet there was still the pressure of having to create something new when the palette had been so comprehensively used to such great effect. This was the songwriter who George Martin had apparently described as the greatest of his generation. Everything pointed to taking some time out, even if the Mustique demos suggested that he still hadn't lost his touch. But whether he was encouraged to keep going or just couldn't stop, he continued working without a break and *Be Here Now* seemed to evolve almost of its own accord.

'The songs just kind of grew and grew,' said Brine, 'and we were experimenting with lots of amps and pedals and seeing how far we could push the layers .... [Noel] really got some great guitar sounds on that record. He spent a lot of time going through the mass of amps and pedals.' An incredibly loud monitoring system was used to listen back to the recording as it progressed, another indication of how everything was becoming more overwhelming. It was almost as if the act of putting together an album had become some kind of macho test of strength – how much could everyone take?

Many of the elements that had made Oasis so strong now counted against them. Gallagher had always had overall control of what happened and with the earlier albums that had helped define Oasis's musical character. Now he had the budget to do exactly what he wanted but there was nobody in place to act as a counter balance. Co-producer Owen Morris had done so much on *Definitely Maybe* to pare it back to basics but he was now working with Gallagher to ladle as many guitars as possible onto the tracks.

When things were calmer many years later, in 2012, Gallagher would have a markedly more considered view of why he did what he did. 'Music is a thing that changes people's lives. It has the capacity to make young people's lives better. Music got us through school, break-ups, whatever - so it's more than just entertainment, the way I see it.' At the time of writing *Be Here Now* his band were in the middle of the storm and he had no real reason to consider why he was compelled to produce more songs, but from what he later said it seemed to be something that was fundamental to him, whatever else was going on around him. 'It's like, if you can write it, you should do. You've got a duty to the world to put it fucking out there. There's not enough good things in the world. You've not got a duty to make more guns, or synthesise more drugs, or fucking design more cars. But you've got a duty to make music. If you can, you should.'

So the results of that compulsion could be patchy and it was almost inevitable that with the circumstances around the making of *Be Here Now* they would be. But in themselves, the full-on party that characterised so much of the band's life at the time was only a representation of where they were at the time. Gallagher wasn't really doing anything in his music that he hadn't before, in that he had always written about the world as he found it. As any songwriter who draws on personal experience must find, the more successful he became, the harder it was to connect with the ordinary fan. 'I tried to do that with *Be Here Now* and it was all champagne and supermodels,' he later said, 'and who wants to hear that when they're on their way to work?'

The lyrics on previous albums hadn't been that much more relevant though and Gallagher would regularly say on completion of an album that he'd just decided the words 'would do' and that the next one would be different. It was as if lyrics were designed to fill the spaces around the music and for someone who was writing on his own, that was enough. The difference, he would later say, was that he now had the same attitude to the album as a whole. In 2001 he said, '"Well, fuck it, that'll do," which is what *Be Here Now* should have been called.' Something had been lost in translation between Mustique and the English countryside but while critics and many fans would soon come to the same conclusion, it would be unfair to overlook the album entirely.

While the sheer loudness of the guitars overwhelmed tracks such as 'My Big Mouth', there were more inventive moments. 'Magic Pie' has often been cited as one of the least successful tracks to define *Be Here Now*, yet there was a charm about the song and a quiet authority to Gallagher's vocals that set it apart from the gale that blew through much of the rest of the album. The psychedelic tinge gave it a much-needed sense of playfulness, though the keyboard itself had been something of an accident. 'The jazzy bit at the end is played on a Mellotron which was made for the Beatles' *Abbey Road* sessions,' Gallagher said. 'All I did was run my elbows across the keys and this mad jazz came out and everyone laughed.'

There were also the horns of 'Don't Go Away', in a reference to the sound of Gallagher's hero Burt Bacharach and strings elsewhere, all arranged by Gallagher. Here again was an astute awareness of different textures and moods which varied the album. 'I tried to keep them as simple as possible. I like the way Marc Bolan used them on "Children of the Revolution". People do remember string parts as separate hooklines, you know. You just don't want to use them slushily.'

Slush would not be used by many to describe *Be Here Now*, from the confrontational opening of 'D'You Know

What I Mean?' onwards. Gallagher was well aware of how generalised the title was and the call to arms in the chorus. For someone who was careful not to give away too much in his lyrics, he seemed to know just the effect he wanted to achieve. 'Very vague, very ambiguous, that'll do,' he said. 'Look in the mirror and wink while you're singing it and it's quite saucy.' Religious imagery frequently cropped up in Gallagher's lyrics, ready sources of big and easily understandable messages for someone so wedded to anthemic numbers and 'D'You Know What I Mean?' kicked off *Be Here Now* with some choice examples of Gallagher's ongoing dialogue with the Almighty. 'On Judgement day, if there ever is one, I'll have a few things to say to that cunt,' said Gallagher, though as usual he was quick not to impose a particular interpretation on his words. 'I'm usually pissed when I'm writing, or stoned, so it could be about fuck all, really. Who knows?' Elsewhere he called them his best lyrics though even as he did he seemed, however flippantly, to feel some uncertainty about them. 'Saying that, they wouldn't have to be much cop to beat some of my fucking lyrics, would they? It's all about cultural images, more than anything.'

Then there were the tracks which had a more earthly inspiration. 'Meg is "The Girl in the Dirty Shirt",' he told *Q* magazine. 'We were doing a gig in Brighton just before Meg and me were going out. She was at the hotel ironing a dirty shirt because she hadn't brought enough clothes with her. I know it sounds a bit soft.' It was welcome though, as there were far fewer light-hearted moments than there had been on the previous albums. *Be Here Now* was later widely categorised as the ultimate coke-fuelled album but just as much – and perhaps indistinguishable – was the sense in the long, noisy tracks it carried of the place that the band now occupied in rock'n'roll. This, Gallagher said, would mark the end of the first part of his master plan for his band. He would go on to talk about how he was determined to strip the band's sound down and rebuild it before they returned to the studio – which would not be for almost two years.

Unable to make it to the *Be Here Now* recording at all was Johnny Depp, whose slide guitar from the 'Fade In-Out' Mustique demo ended up being used on the final version. Gallagher said, 'I don't think 14-year-old girls will be skipping about to this one – "'Ere, Shelle, wind that one on will yer!" – until they find out Johnny Depp's on it. It's going to be weird how that's perceived, having a Hollywood star on the album. But I'm glad it happened. If he hadn't been around, we'd have had to get some fat old geezer who'd be telling us about how he played with Clapton in '76 and did a slide solo that lasted for fucking months.'

But despite Gallagher's admiration for post-punk brevity, it was not one of the qualities most obvious in the finished album. He finally got to listen back to the thing in all its snarling, overwrought splendour. 'My reaction was, "This is fucking long",' he later said of those 71 minutes. 'I didn't realize how long it was. It's a long fucking record. And then I looked at the artwork, and it had all the song titles with all the times for each track, and none of them seemed to be under six minutes. So then I was like, "Fucking hell. What's going on there?"' But it was done. And four months after recording, the album was released.

That June, Gallagher and Meg Mathews married in Las Vegas. As with everything else around Noel at the time, their relationship had been played out in the press and she found herself a celebrity in her own right, her life under the microscope and the hysteria around the band at such a level that, particularly between albums when news was in short supply, stories were constantly being made up about what they were supposed to have been up to. The wedding was not going to take down the intensity of the scrutiny but Gallagher was used to the coverage. 'You get enough money to do what we do and if that's the price, a little snidey story here and there, then so be it.' Never short on insight, Gallagher himself was the first to say that he was hardly likely to go running to a judge to protect his character when he was constantly providing the press with enough quotes of outrage to keep them churning out features all year long.

On 7 July 'D'You Know What I Mean?' was released. It had been around for a while in various forms since the previous May. 'I had the chords for about a year,' said Gallagher. 'I did it at soundchecks on the acoustic guitar, although the melody was totally different.' It had been the last song to be recorded and came with the full weight of the band's sessions in the studio. In a very indirect way, the song was a nod to Gallagher's early interest in hip hop, in that it sampled the drums from a track on the NWA album *Straight Outta Compton*. He had bought the album almost a decade earlier in 1988. 'I remember when me and the original engineer, Mark Coyle, used to do dance stuff years ago,' he said, 'we put those drums on a track for about half an hour because we thought it was so amazing. Just the pace and the sound of it.' Almost as popular was b-side 'Stay Young', quickly a fan favourite and a track that was sometimes given radio airtime over the more unwieldy lead song.

Oasis-mania was in full swing again with the album now feverishly anticipated but, even as Gallagher was interviewed the week before the single's release, he seemed to be reining back on his usual enthusiastic sales pitch. 'I just wish the rest of the album sounded like that,' he said to the *NME*. 'It's good, but the next one will be better.' This was a different note from Noel Gallagher. Previously, he had always been relentlessly confident about what he was producing and in the early days his claims for greatness had often been dismissed as hyperbole by a new artist who didn't have the grace to adopt the effacing ways of the indie artists. But as he was once proved entirely correct in the reverent way Oasis would eventually be received, the same thing was now happening in reverse. Just when he should be at his most swaggering, he was unusually cautious. And this time he was also not taken serious by a press now used to his entertaining ways. The *NME* journalist wrote of their encounter, 'Well, the guitarist is a bit grumpy right now. He'll cheer up later with the assistance of a couple of Orange Hoochs though.' In Gallagher's amused and amusing approach to press, it was easy to miss the kernel of seriousness in what he said. It was just as true when he was being self-critical as when he had been self-aggrandising. Long before the general reassessment of the album, he was beginning to have doubts.

Management company Ignition were also alarmed at the hype surrounding the new release, but for different reasons. They could just see the whole thing spiralling entirely out of control and tightly restricted first information and then access to listening to it. It was one of the last build-ups of its kind. The internet age would make that impossible, with its leaks, trailers and the immediate release online of any soundchecking of a new song. Ignition were also insistent that record company Creation were as security conscious. One employee claimed that Ignition checked the phones because they thought they might be bugged by the *Sun*, an allegation that after the Murdoch hacking inquiry seems not so much over-sensitivity but simply a normal working day. Yet Ignition's attempt to manage a nation's expectations backfired, serving only to increase the anticipation for the record.

BBC Radio 1's *Evening Session*, presented by Steve Lamacq, was told it could broadcast three tracks on one night shortly before release and five the following night. Lamacq was instructed to bookend the tracks by talking or even play a jingle in the middle of the songs so that they couldn't be bootlegged. 'I've never believed that these badly copied advance tapes actually damage sales that much,' Lamacq wrote in his book *Going Deaf for a Living*, but he did as he was told and spoke over the songs. He hadn't done enough for Ignition, who withheld the other tracks. 'I ended up back on air,' he wrote, 'apologising to listeners again for not coming up with the promised goods. We got a further two tracks, but that was it. It was all very messy.'

Anticipation continued to build and all semblance at playing it cool went with the free but unimaginably valuable publicity of the *Right Here, Right Now* BBC 1 documentary which went out on 20 August, the night before the album went on sale. The date of release itself was unmissable, being inscribed in a calendar used as one of the props on the album cover which also featured the band staring out from the poolside of a country mansion.

As with much of the artwork done over the course of the first three albums, *Be Here Now*'s jacket was done by Brian Cannon and his Microdot design company. The original idea had been to photograph each member of Oasis in a different location around the world and create a montage, but even when they settled on staying at home, they composed the image without the aid of digital manipulation – down to using a crane to lower a real Rolls Royce into position. 'That car is in that pool,' Cannon later said. 'It was scrapped with no engine and it cost us a grand. And all the props around the pool have no meaning whatsoever, I just took Liam and Noel down to a BBC props warehouse in White City [west London] and they picked loads of random stuff, it was total nonsense.'

Be Here Now had landed, setting out its stall by becoming the fastest-selling album in UK chart history, with over 660,000 copies bought in two days, some 350,000 on the first day alone. By 7 September they had reached a million. The critical reception was, initially, far better than it had been for *(What's the Story?) Morning Glory*. Perhaps some commentators were anxious not to underestimate another Oasis album which might catch the public's imagination as they had done with the previous outings. Others seemed to see a brave new world forming before them with *Mojo*'s Charles Shaar Murray overwhelmed: 'It arrives in your living-room like the Grand Canyon, built to scale, constructed entirely out of road-scuffed Marshall stacks and covered in mud. The first time you play it, it's all too much for you to take.' And in what became the best-known line of the review he added, 'Dem a come fe mess up de area *serious*.'

The general tone of the album's reception would be largely entirely reversed when the dust of the launch settled. *Spin* would go to find its good points surrounded by flab and *Q* decided in an anniversary issue ten years on, that 'so colossally did *Be Here Now* fall short of expectations that it killed Brit Pop', a claim as excitable as any of the music on the record. Yet Gallagher seemed to agree in no small part. While he was usually most enthusiastic about his most recent record, he could be relied upon to reassess his opinions of his past work with time. But he never expressed much fondness for *Be Here Now* after the initial push had faded. 'I won't bullshit you, we'd fucked everything up by then and we blew it.' He was beginning to head towards that conclusion fairly early on and it wasn't only the *NME* who got to hear it.

Towards the end of the promotional round, long after the *Evening Session* non-plays, the Radio 1 programme heard that Gallagher wanted to do an interview. This was big news, as the normally garrulous Gallaghers had been noticeably quiet as part of the campaign of secrecy. 'Considering the grief that had gone before,' Steve Lamacq wrote, 'I suppose we should have just gaily waved two fingers at their radio plugger.' But they couldn't turn down what turned out to be both of the biggest stars in the country as Liam came along too. The brothers sparred brilliantly in their first joint interview since the 1994 encounter that had been issued as a single. Nobody was off limits – from those around them in the radio studio that night, to other musicians and each other. It was vintage stuff.

Yet there were almost wistful notes from Noel. 'Work's become boring, mate,' he said at one point. Asked if he was feeling down, he said, 'Yeah. Everything that led up to Knebworth was really special. Now we've just become another band.' Liam left before the interview ended and his brother returned to the theme. 'It's not that the band have become boring or anything like that... it's sort of not exciting any more. And he [Liam] would disagree.' Lamacq asked if that made it harder. 'Well, we are the establishment, I understand that,' said Gallagher, saying elsewhere in the discussion, 'I don't know what I'm going to write next time, but if I can't do something that excites me, then I could possibly never do another album. But I need, mentally, time off.' This was exactly what the band weren't going to get. But Lamacq's revealing interview did point the way to how things would be as the Be Here Now tour formed an end point for this first part of Oasis's career.

Following a handful of US dates in June, the global slog began in earnest that September in Europe and finished in Mexico the following spring, including another stand at Earls Court in London. Support on the tour included Travis and Ocean Colour Scene, further underlining the connection between the two bands. Playing the new album out was even more exhausting than promoting *(What's the Story) Morning Glory?* and embodied all the excesses and pitfalls of life on the road. If, as Gallagher had suggested on Radio 1, it had all got a bit predictable, their hedonistic attitude to the tour kept the excitement up as it had done in the studio. Nothing would be quite the same after this tour and Noel Gallagher certainly wouldn't be. It was the tour as much as the experience of recording the album which would lead him to reassess his approach to his life and begin to take down the volume. But for now, wherever in the world Oasis turned up, they were still playing and then causing chaos.

As on the previous tour, Liam had to pull out of some shows due to problems with his voice and Noel would take over singing duties. It was also on this tour that journalist Paulo Hewitt noted Gallagher being called The Chief with real reverence. 'He saw how everyone was so careful to tread softly around him,' Hewitt later wrote. '"Chief" this, "Chief" that. "Got you this, Chief", got you that. Noel basked in our absolute acquiescence to him.'

Gallagher reintroduced his acoustic part of the show during the tour, when he would go out solo to perform classics like 'Stand by Me'. But for the most part, the shows embodied the pile-driving approach that had characterised the studio sessions. The stage set throughout took its cue from the grand design of the album artwork, including the clock, a telephone booth from which the band would emerge and a Rolls Royce drum riser. This was what rock'n'roll was all about, the concept seemed to say but that was fine, as neither the band nor their audience were in the mood for subtlety. One review of the Earls Court nights memorably described how even the bartenders around the cavernous venue joined the fans in a lusty rendition of the 'Don't Look Back in Anger' chorus.

Yet there were quieter moments. It was before one of the three nights at Earls Court that Gallagher unexpectedly gave each member of the band a scooter he'd bought for them in Italy. Photographer Jill Furmanovsky remembered them all riding at top speed around the – fortunately sizeable – backstage area. They did an impromptu photo shoot in front of the ageing but iconic venue, all of Oasis sat on their brand new scooters below giant posters of the brothers, the pictures also shot by Furmanovsky. 'I had the camera on motordrive and I shot off two rolls,' she later said, explaining how they had to dash off before the fans got to them. 'Luckily, they came out perfectly. Looking back, it was terribly exciting; that's the whole point about Oasis. It's nerve-wracking to shoot something that moves as fast as they do.'

The start of 1998 was greeted by a mid-tour single from the album, 'All Around the World'. This was another that had been in Gallagher's treasure chest for a while – it had been held off the first album because he felt at the time he couldn't do it justice. Even now he had trimmed three minutes off, though at nine minutes it was very much in keeping with the rest of the album. And despite his reservations about *Be Here Now*, he could still talk songs up when he wanted. 'Now we can get away with the 36-piece orchestra. And the longer the better as far as I'm concerned. If it's good ... But there are three key changes towards the end. Imagine how much better "Hey Jude" would have been with three key changes towards the end. I like the ambition of it, all that time ago. What was all that about when we didn't even have our first single out?'

The furious light of the band continued to attract celebrity fans, among them ubiquitous England football star Paul Gascoigne, who had become a friend of Gallagher and who, along with his friend Jimmy – who had found a kind of fame as 'five bellies' – hung out with the band. Oasis had come to define a sort of laddish pop which fitted in with the cultural temperature of the times and their social life, with Gascoigne and the likes of DJ and presenter Chris Evans, were still reported on a seemingly daily basis in the media. Then there were other celebrity fans such as Naomi Campbell who, like the band, was someone from an ordinary background who had made it and in a way had more success than they knew what to do with.

Out in the US Oasis also met up again with Johnny Depp. Paulo Hewitt, who had accompanied the band on tour, recorded how Gallagher and his brother partied at Depp's house. Appropriately enough, this was the former residence of Dracula actor Bela Lugosi. Guests included legendary producer Rick Rubin and producer and A&R man George Drakoulias. Gallagher entertained the room with an impromptu performance of an unnamed new song, singing and playing guitar for the exclusive crowd. This was just another night out for Gallagher, while for Paulo Hewitt it ended sometime in the following day after they visited Smashing Pumpkins in the studio and, as Gallagher whirled off with singer Billy Corgan on a fresh mad mission, Hewitt returned to his hotel room – 'watching the world spin around and around. And on and on. And so on.'

Gallagher's drive remained and his talent was undimmed, yet there had been no real reason for him to try and outdo *(What's the Story?) Morning Glory*. It was only in trying to keep pace with the band's image in the press by setting out to do

Top: Noel playing with Oasis at the Point Theatre, Dublin, in 2005.

Bottom: Noel posing for a portrait in Sydney, Australia, in 2005.

With Chris Martin, front man of Coldplay, at the 2005 *Q* Awards.

Top left: In deep conversation with Paul Weller at the *Q* Awards.

Top right: Noel posing with the prestigious O2 Silver Clef Award for contribution to the music industry, July 2008.

Bottom: Back to the old days: the original Oasis line-up in 1994.

Top: Noel performing with Oasis at Wembley Stadium in October 2008.

Bottom: Members of Oasis pose on the Wembley pitch just before the launch of their UK stadium tour of 2009.

Top left: Noel and Kinks frontman Ray Davies at the *GQ* awards 2010.

Top right: With Lily Allen in 2010 for the *GQ* awards.

Bottom: Posing with fellow guests Miranda Hart and Michael Sheen after filming for *The Jonathan Ross Show* in 2011.

One the red carpet with girlfriend Sara MacDonald and daughter Anaïs.

Top: Noel Gallagher's High Flying Birds perform live at Alcatraz, Milan, Italy in November 2011. Noel formed the band in 2011 and it is made up of a selection of rock talent including Mike Rowe (former Oasis session pianist), Jeremy Stacey (formerly of The Lemon Trees) and Russell Pritchard (from The Zutons).

Bottom right: Taking a hit at the O2 Silver Clef awards with Ricky Hatton, former boxer, in 2008.

Bottom left: Noel at the 2011 *Q* awards with Tom Meighan (*centre*) of Kasabian and Jessie J (*right*) where Noel won the *Q* Icon award.

In March 2013 Noel got together with Damon Albarn (left) and Graham Coxon of Blur at the Teenage Cancer Trust concerts he curated at London's Royal Albert Hall. Emphatically burying Brit Pop's most famous feud, they performed Blur's 'Tender' with Paul Weller on drums.

that which had made *Be Here Now* pale by comparison. And as the album sold something in the region of eight million copies worldwide – although it peaked fairly soon after release – it was in itself hardly a disaster. In a way, said Gallagher later, it was probably just as well that the beast that was *Be Here Now* had been a bit of a wake-up call rather than just made them even bigger. 'What would we have done the next time?' he later asked.

It was only when he was speaking as the High Flying Birds got into their stride in 2011 that he seemed finally to have the way he needed to work more figured out. 'What I realised, only recently, is that you can still write about emotions because they're the same for every man and woman ... if I could write another *Definitely Maybe*, fucking hell, man, I would. But all of these things are just fleeting moments. You catch them and they're gone.'

CHAPTER 8

THE MASTER PLAN

'I'VE GOT A CERTAIN STYLE AND I'VE GOT NO CONTROL
OVER WHAT I WRITE. I'M NOT TECHNICALLY PROFICIENT
ENOUGH TO ATTEMPT ALL KINDS OF MUSIC. I WISH I COULD
WRITE A FUCKING RECORD LIKE *RAW POWER* OR *WISH
YOU WERE HERE* OR HAVE THE ABILITY OF A MUSICAL
CHAMELEON. BUT FUCK IT, I'M NOT. I JUST WRITE
THESE SONGS BECAUSE THEY'RE REAL TO ME.'
NOEL GALLAGHER IN 2011

Kelly Jones, frontman with Stereophonics, saw how
deceptively easy Noel Gallagher made it look to be a
superstar. 'Coming up off the back of the Brit Pop thing and
getting to know people like Noel and stuff,' Jones said in
2007, 'you realised that it is all about song-writing and it's
about working your bollocks off, but having a good time
and making it look like it's easy, while behind the scenes
putting the graft in.'

Stereophonics had came to prominence towards the end

of the 1990s with *Word Gets Around*, when Oasis had done their bit to make traditional guitar music attractive again, and Jones was in a position to see Gallagher's sleight of hand act at close quarters. For all Oasis's well-publicised chaos, Gallagher was not only talented but hard working and one of the sharpest minds in the music business. But the 1990s was characterised by a hedonism which brought with it suspicion of anything that seemed to try too hard.

The mood of the times was a rebuttal to the politicised 1980s, when indie guitar bands had been identified with the left wing and the hangover from the punk explosion which regarded success and conspicuous wealth as inherently suspect. But although fading recession in the early 1990s came too late to rescue Prime Minister John Major, the new sense of prosperity made an earnest attitude to doing anything creative seem deeply unfashionable. The previous decade in indie rock was seen as having become obsessed with a colourless opposition to the unstoppable Tories and now there was a bit more money and the dance explosion had shown a different sensibility. Coming out of working class Manchester, Noel Gallagher felt that sense of wanting more out of life as much as anyone in the country. He was by nature and environment a Labour man – nobody could have been bought up in his neighbourhood and thanked Margaret Thatcher – but it was the Conservative sense of individualism which drove him to succeed. When an interviewer pointed out that for someone who declared themselves to be non-political, his songs were about positive energy and going out to do something, he said, 'Of course! But Oasis was about people changing their lives for themselves.' This was something that the Thatcherite wing of the Conservatives would have understood.

Perhaps this was Thatcher's least tangible legacy. For the first time in years it was okay to go for success on its own terms, but although Gallagher saw making it with Oasis as an end in itself he simultaneously shunned careerism in the music industry and was always very scornful of musicians who had seen the life as just another job. He could tell you how many millions of copies Oasis had shifted, but he was careful to say that he was not one of those who was on the phone to his record company all the time demanding to know how well this week in the charts was going. 'What a lot of people fail to understand is that we never started this band as a career move ... this is our life,' he said. 'We never asked for a record deal, someone gave us one. We never asked for fucking 20 million record sales, it just came.'

But once they did, he was determined to enjoy it. Gallagher was pragmatic about his circumstances despite his pride at his working class roots. He enjoyed living in London and he seemed comfortable existing in the highest reaches of the music business. It was all part of his ease operating in the media. 'I came from a shithole in Manchester, right,' he told the *Guardian* in 2006, 'so it was all brilliant to me. Even touring in a transit van was better than being in my flat. Then when we got a deal, we were like, "Bring it on!" I wanted the big hairdo, big shades, big car, big house, swimming pool, jet, drug habit, a mirrored top hat and a chimp. All of it. The Kasabian lads told me they'd only get out of bed to read about us in the paper. And what would you rather read? "The guy from Keane's been to a rabbit sanctuary because one of the rabbits needed a kidney implant, so he swapped his with it", or "Liam Gallagher sets fire to a policeman in cocaine madness, while his brother Noel runs down Oxford Street nude"?'

And he was upfront about the benefits success brought and what it meant for his family. 'I want her to be Prime Minister,' he once said when Anaïs, his daughter with Meg Mathews, was very small. 'And you have to go to a posh school for that.'

The lack of embarrassment about the trappings of success in Gallagher reflected a wider change in culture. While pop music had never needed to signify anything weighty to capture an audience – *Smash Hits* had spent much of the 1980s celebrating that very fact – indie rock had set great store about being somehow more important. Oasis would be at the vanguard of music for which that was no longer true. This was happening as the industry was becoming more professionalised and being a rock star was no longer solely the preserve of the outlaw. As the growing internet made information about bands ever easier to find, the life of a touring band became steadily demystified.

The same was true in other areas of creativity. The alternative comics of the 1980s, with their stern anti-sexism, politicised views were fast becoming the establishment and they were followed by acts who adopted the attitude but not the polemic. As with the indie musicians, the likes of David Baddiel and Frank Skinner were bringing the fringes of the Comedy Store in London to the forefront of mainstream TV. On shows such as *TFI Friday*, the likes of Chris Evans were introducing rock and edgy comics to a national audience. Panel shows sprang up all over the place and with a show such as *They Think It's All Over*, with Nick Hancock on BBC 1 from 1995, barriers between the previously separate areas of sport and humour began to come down. It would be the same with music. There was still a general sense of attitude and a light-hearted notion of rebellion, but seriousness was not so cool. As long as it came couched with irony, it was more acceptable to play around with the idea of what had rather dismissively come to be called political correctness.

The same celebratory approach was to be found in the art world. The movement dubbed the Young British Artists (YBA) – Damien Hirst, Tracy Emin, the Chapman brothers and others championed by collector Charles Saatchi – were as outrageous and excessive as anything in rock'n'roll. There was a great humour and verve to their work, which was big, bold and made national headlines in the Sensation exhibition at the Royal Academy in London that opened a month after *Be Here Now* was released. There was little to be seen here that required interpretation or was burdened with metaphor. The UK had long expressed itself most profoundly through literature but here were other mediums

– art, music, comedy – that absorbed the struggles of the 1980s and embraced its entrepreneurial aspects at the same time. It was daring but not difficult. And as was allegedly demonstrated in the aftermath of the death of Princess Diana, also in the crowded late summer of 1997, the British public were finding a collective emotion that had apparently not been tapped before.

No more obvious was this new freedom of expression than in what became known as the new lad. With monthly men's magazines such as *Loaded* starting in the early 1990s, the more sensitive 'new man' was replaced by his earthier, less responsible younger brother, who was into girls, football and liked a laugh. By the late 1990s, *Loaded* alone was shifting nearly half a million copies a month under its strapline 'For men who should know better'. In truth, men had probably not changed substantially in those few years, but it was suddenly not only acceptable to voice those views, but actively encouraged. New lads under new Labour blossomed – it wasn't something confined to one section of the population. Working class, middle class; female as well as male, there was a feeling of hedonism which was tangible even far away from the self-appointed taste makers of the capital.

As much as this was a usefully sympathetic backdrop for Oasis as they began to make their name, it was nothing more than coincidence. Noel Gallagher was articulate, direct and ambitious but he had never tried to fit in with what was happening more widely in the times. It was simply never a

sturm und drang. 'I don't think two blokes having the same fucking argument for 16 years over and over is the stuff of opera. *Oasis: the Opera* would be very short. The fat lady would refuse to sing it.'

Yet there was a curiously defensive tone to his frequent needling of Radiohead and Blur. As justifiably proud as he was of his unpretentious song-writing and the direct line he had to millions of fans, it was as if he felt, despite the way his anthems connected with so many people, that he had to attack the competition. It was almost as if he needed to defend the merit of his work. When he once talked about having watched a *South Bank Show* featuring Blur he seemed to be most exercised by Damon Albarn talking of having not got through his A-level in music. The way Gallagher spoke about it, it wasn't so much that he hadn't done a similar exam, but that a fellow star would admit to having studied music. 'You play one chord on a fucking guitar and you're a musician – end of fucking story. People slag us off for it but it's a proper emotional thing. It's a human playing a tree.'

Gallagher's own abilities were never in doubt. While Damon Albarn's many side projects and diversions got a lot of press, Gallagher's song-writing skills and even remixing advice was highly prized. Collaborations in both writing and recording collaborations were commonplace for him, so much so that some of them didn't even see the light of day. By the mid-1990s he was knocking around with as different artists as former Lemonhead Evan Dando and

Death in Vegas's Richard Fearless but didn't release the work they produced together. He was hardly desperate for opportunities.

But in the way he would often poke gentle fun at Radiohead, it was almost as if he was considering how it would be to be quite so experimental. Radiohead had been on the unsigned bill at In The City in 1992 alongside Oasis but they were never seen as Brit Pop contenders in the same way. And yet Gallagher would point out any fault line in the cerebral Oxford band's career, however tenuous. 'All the anarchists and Thom Yorkes of this world,' Gallagher said of disillusionment with government, 'who are like, "All politicians are baaaad" – they reckon they've been trying to destroy politics for years.'

He had a very definite idea of what constituted authenticity which he sometimes seemed as constrained by as he was proud of. An authentic sound was a four or five piece band with at least two guitars. But although he was criticised in the early days of Oasis for the direct influence in his work of other bands, it was a charge he would himself later level at a new wave of guitar bands in turn. Just as he had a very traditional view of how acts should behave in rock'n'roll, later groups would take inspiration from the way that Oasis had approached the music industry. But for Gallagher there was a difference. 'We meant it, but I just look at some of these fuckers and think, Do you really think that, though? Do you really think you're that great?' he told

NME. 'I think a lot of these bands are – not fake – but just copying the blueprint.'

When it came to the actual content of songs, Gallagher had always been open about the influences on his own writing. He was most succinct and relaxed on the subject when addressing tabloid rumours that he was going to sue *Popstars* winners Hear'Say over similarities between 2001's 'Pure and Simple' and *Be Here Now*'s 'All Around the World'. 'Come on mate, us?' he said to a *Q* writer. 'Are we really going to sue a band for making a record that sounds like someone else's? I don't think so.'

While Gallagher attracted comment on the amount that his work owed to earlier musicians, it was hardly a new phenomenon. There has always been a long tradition of appropriating music that was created by earlier composers. The stars of the 1960s who were pioneering rock music often did so by taking old blues and folk numbers and making them their own. Almost all of the artists that can be heard in Gallagher's work – the Beatles, the Rolling Stones, Led Zeppelin – had done the same kind of thing in their time, but it was how they used what they found that made it their own. Perhaps the main difference was that by the time that Noel Gallagher was writing it was easier to tell where the original had come from whereas many of his own heroes had been listening to artists who had disappeared or fallen out of fashion. It was harder to disguise that for a Noel Gallagher and to begin with in his own brand of inspirational anthem he didn't try. The very familiarity was part of their appeal, yet as his writing developed over the years he moved on to a more subtle and intimate style of music.

His approach to lyrics was more consistent. He talked in interview of how they were the last element to come together in his tracks and even into the High Flying Birds they seemed to be set for a purpose rather than an end in their own right. He kept them non-specific and was rarely a story teller in his music. Sometimes the lines were non-sequiturs, but that didn't matter when the overall impact, the mood of the song, was what counted. Characters spun through his lines, the Sallies and the Elsas, and such was his facility with emphasis that these brief mentions seemed to signify so much more. They were mere suggestions of sketches yet somehow it often seemed like a whole person was revealed, even when little more than a name had been mentioned.

But mostly, at least in the early days, the words were framed by the stadium swagger of the music. There was the frequent use of religious imagery which might have tied in with his Irish Catholic background, yet in the context of his particular way of working, he would say himself it was more generally used for effect. He would make the occasional gnomic comment regarding religion – 'there's only one soul mate and that's the man upstairs,' he told Q when he was asked about his views on marriage following his split with Meg Mathews – but he was more usually dismissive of questions of faith. If he was given to introspection, he never shared it in interview. His persona for the press was generally upbeat, funny, acerbic and keenly aware of his audience and what he would expect if it was him listening to or reading about his favourite artist.

It was if much of what remained absent from his songs he poured into his encounters with the media. His songs were rarely funny in the way that his soundbites could be, he was full of pithy and revealing anecdotes when he was revved up in a promotional tour. Interviewers would find him ready to point out the ridiculous aspects of being a star, the small indignities that punctured the image of Noel Gallagher as rock titan, as if nobody should think he was getting above himself or that he was trying too hard to be somebody important.

There was the time he was asked by a hotel waiter delivering room service if he could sign a CD. A brilliantly observed slapstick routine was relayed with all the tension and embarrassment of some classic sitcom: 'Now he had suit trousers on, you know, like what hotel people wear? And you know the back pocket in them trousers? It's basically a slit in the arse. Well, fucking somehow, this guy's got a CD in there and it's fucking stuck… So I'm stood there looking at me breakfast and he's pulling at the back of his trousers but the CD's not coming. And he's starting to sweat. And I end up round the back of the trousers but he's there yanking too. So I'm going to him, "Look, mate, just relax – let it all out!" Anyway, this goes on longer than it should until in the end I just grab him by the fucking shoulders and say, "Stop!" And finally I manage to edge it out of him...' The punchline is Gallagher's exasperation when the waiter reveals he doesn't even want the autograph for himself.

Noel Gallagher was always a master of misdirection. When many were saying the way he talked up his songs to begin with was nothing more than bluster, he was being serious. And much later, as his music became more focused and its rousing aggression subsided into something more still, he was taken far more seriously when he was at his most relaxed and witty. But through everything, the hectic Brit Pop years, the considered later Oasis albums and after the split, the songs themselves endured when many thought they wouldn't. Almost two decades after *Definitely Maybe* and his songbook has become part of the history of music in the way he was always certain it would do. There might have been a certain inevitability in 'Wonderwall' being selected from all his songs for the closing ceremony of the 2012 London Olympics, but who would have predicted even that in the mid-1990s? There could only be so far that any musician could get on good fortune and buoyant times without the talent telling over time. But at the beginning, Gallagher had something to prove. With a tested catalogue to his name his continued delight in producing music continues to show just how deeply his passion runs. That was perhaps more the mark of authenticity than anything else.

'I'm going to set the benchmark,' he said as the High

Flying Birds got under way. 'A year from now there will be a benchmark and it might be down by my ankles or it might be way above my head. It may exceed everyone's expectations or it may just be all right. It may just be another album. Don't know yet. But that's the great thing about it. Who knows?'

CHAPTER 9

TO BE FREE

The riotous, hedonistic storm that erupted in Gallagher's life and reached its zenith around the release of *Be Here Now* had calmed. Not that things were any more certain: both professionally and personally his life was about to face a series of upheavals. Some familiar faces were about to depart, but there would also be some positive new arrivals, one of which would make Gallagher happier than he had ever been before.

Oasis had continued touring in support of *Be Here Now* into early 1998 and the headlines that had dogged them in the UK came along for the ride. There was trouble on the plane from Hong Kong to Perth and airline Cathay Pacific were reported to be thinking of banning them. The press abroad took on the job of covering their every move and the band found Australia was quite hostile. To relieve the pressure, Guigsy organised a football match in a local park. The media turned up to see Gallagher put in a good show, hanging back and telling everyone else what to do.

By the time the Be Here Now tour finally juddered to a halt in the spring, Gallagher was on the way to becoming a more sober person – in every respect. Back home, as the year went on he took a good look around him and realised he didn't know half the people who seemed to have taken up permanent residence in Supernova Heights. Friends of friends would be sat around the kitchen and he had no idea who they were. He later explained his reasoning. 'Cocaine itself isn't that bad. It just makes you drink more and that's the worst drug there is. Especially when you're surrounded by people whose psychosis sets in the more they drink. But people think I stood up at a party and announced, "That was my last line of cocaine, from this day forth I shall take no more," and everybody sighed and left. It wasn't like that. The reason I packed it in was that it was only meant to be a weekend, which became a week, which became a month and so on. I just decided I couldn't be arsed any more."

It was, it seemed, as simple as that. Gallagher's grounded persona was not just a stage act. Not for him the endless shuttling from clinic to fresh drugs hell. He just seemed to find it very easy to step back from the endless partying. He wasn't alone, as others in the Brit Pop first division were beginning to come to similar conclusions. It wasn't just partying – the trappings that colossal success brought were not what the likes of Blur and Pulp had imagined. Everyone, it seemed, was waking up to a new Labour hangover. It had seemed that Gallagher himself was unshakeable, that however much gusto he applied to ticking off items on the rock'n'roll clipboard of excess, he could still record an entire album later that night. But he had even suffered from panic attacks in the year or so previously. It had been Meg Mathews who would talk him down until the middle of one night when he got up and wrote out his feelings in what would become 'Gas Panic!' on the next album.

The most symbolic indication of Gallagher's disenchantment with how things were going came when the couple relocated to the countryside outside London and Supernova Heights was eventually sold to 'one of the girls from Hollyoaks,' as he later said. He laughed off the rumours that he took the garish sign above the door with him. 'I didn't bother. I couldn't be arsed with all that. The house was like a bad advert for drugs if you went inside it. Fucking hell, man. There was a 17-foot fish tank in one wall with one fish in it.' Having only really known Manchester and London, the change of pace had an immediate effect on the urban boy.

He had few regrets. Nobody had enjoyed acting out the rock dream more than Gallagher. It was in every Oasis lyric and every chord change up to *Be Here Now*. 'Don't forget,' he later said, 'Before I was even in a band … I was a roadie for three years with Inspiral Carpets. What do you think I was doing then? Drinking mineral water and eating Twiglets?' But he also knew he had to approach everything differently. Musically, his role within the band was evolving alongside the other changes in his life. From now on, Oasis albums would feature more vocals from the senior Gallagher. In fact, this trend began even with a retrospective release, when, in November 1998, the band released a compilation album of b-sides, entitled *The Masterplan*. Initially, the release was intended primarily for US and Far East markets, where Oasis b-sides were not officially on the market and only obtainable as costly imports. However, the album became something bigger, not least because of the element of democracy in its track listing. Fans were invited to vote online for the songs they wished to see included. As The Chief was involved, of course, the democracy was limited: Gallagher oversaw the final cut of tracks from the backlist.

More than anything, Gallagher simply loved b-sides as a concept. When he had been a young fan himself he had always appreciated it when bands put effort into providing more than just a mix of a song already available on an album. For him the b-side was a symbol of his ability as a songwriter. He took pride in the fact that he could tuck away tracks of the quality of 'Talk Tonight', 'The Masterplan' and 'Half the World Away'. As far as he was concerned, any other band of the era would have killed for such songs as singles – the choice of 'Half the World Away' for theme to

The Royle Family served only to underline that. When he first played 'The Masterplan' song to Liam, his younger brother said, 'You don't know how fucking good you are,' prompting a moment of genuine shyness in Noel. 'And it's a b-side!' Liam added. 'How fucking top is that?'

B-sides allowed Gallagher to turn down the volume a little and play around with the instrumentation a little more than the singalong choruses expected of an Oasis single. But there was still a certain amount of trademark swagger in the very concept of the compilation. Was he reminding the rest of the music industry that their finest cuts were outclassed by his afterthoughts? Or was it more than that? Did *The Masterplan* showcase Gallagher's centrality to the band's creativity now the band had peaked? Even if it were only coincidental it was striking how many of the songs featured his vocals. But it was an extraordinary catalogue by any standards and the frequently mellow album stands as a potent reminder that, even during the peak of their 'madferit' days, Gallagher was often calmer than the public image might have suggested.

The album reached UK No 2 – a great achievement for a collection of second tracks – and in its first fortnight on sale it sold 300,000 copies in the UK alone. The *NME* declared it an 'Everest to the rest of this year's K2s', awarding it nine out of 10 stars. Highlighting 'Talk Tonight' and the other tracks that Gallagher had written after the 1994 bust-up in America, the music weekly lauded his ability to deliver 'an emotional uppercut when you least expected it'.

But the praise wasn't universal. *Rolling Stone*'s Barney Hoskyns, a veteran music critic, was less impressed, dismissing the album as full of 'bored ballads... leaden rockers [and] listless clichés'. Oasis had been accused of many musical crimes but this was one it was harder to make stand up. If anything, he used his b-sides to break out and play around more with instrumentation and emotion. And the band's next studio album would show his willingness to engage with new ideas by opening with the band's most dance-based track to date. It was a departure from style which had its roots in Gallagher's collaborations with drum-and-bass pioneer Goldie.

Noel had played guitar on the track 'Temper Temper', never an Oasis fan's favourite. It appeared on *Saturnz Return*, the follow-up to 1995's groundbreaking *Timeless* and if it was not the expected thing for Gallagher to do, it was certainly more believable than the idea that in ten years Goldie himself would appear on *Strictly Come Dancing*. As for Gallagher, he was delighted with the results of 'Temper Temper'. 'It's the most disgustingly dirty jungle track I've ever heard,' he said. Some music critics would have been surprised to learn that Gallagher had knowledge of enough jungle tracks, dirty or otherwise, to make such a statement. However, as he reminded the world, 'I used to be a bit of a clubber in me time,' he said with some understatement, 'when I was a kid, down the Haçienda.' There was more banter when he was asked what it was like to work with Goldie. They seemed to have got on really well and Gallagher gently mocked Goldie's acting forays. 'He should stick to music, man. He's a rubbish actor.' The sessions themselves had been 'a nightmare,' he joked. 'You can't understand a word he says and he comes from Wolverhampton.'

The collaboration was no mere nod to current fashions. Both parties seemed genuinely enthused by what they had created. When he played 'Temper Temper' at an Oasis after-show party, Goldie had leaped around with delight. 'Check it, man, check that guitar,' he said of Gallagher's contribution. 'Wild!'

The development in Gallagher's song writing would be felt on the next Oasis studio album. There had been talk of an intriguing glimpse into his earliest forays into writing during the Be Here Now tour when it emerged that someone claiming to know Gallagher put some demo tapes he claimed were Gallagher's up for auction at Christie's. Gallagher refused to get drawn on the matter, though the songs which have subsequently been distributed widely on the internet, were generally believed to be authentic four-track demos from the late 1980s.

However, Goldie wasn't the only contemporary influence on the new Oasis writing. Gallagher had become a big fan of the Beta Band as he was considering and compiling his next major work. Their heavy percussive style, laced with trip hop, would soon be subtly detectable in Oasis. This was more than an unconscious evolution. When Gallagher completed *Be Here Now*, he had told everyone who would listen that he was going to make sure the next studio album would move the Oasis sound on for a new millennium. That was a key reason for him taking his time getting back to recording. For someone known for keeping such a tight rein on every aspect of his output, it was perhaps a surprise that The Chief had considered sending recorded tracks outside of the band's circle to be mixed. He had talked of the studio he had in his home and how he had been experimenting with samples.

Gallagher had been keen to stretch himself, admiring the likes of the Prodigy and Beastie Boys and grasping the opportunity to see how you could work in a different style to produce a bastardised rock sound that was quite unlike anything else. And if this never wholeheartedly translated into a radically new way of doing things in Oasis, incrementally it was having an effect. It would certainly tell when it came to his first solo release.

Perhaps the person he wanted to surprise more than anyone was himself. Following the release of *Be Here Now*, he later said, he had felt he finished more than just a triptych of albums. 'My passion for music had gone somewhat and I was kind of in a different place,' he said. 'I wasn't bothered. I was doing it for the sake of it.' Trying out new sounds was the means by which he began the slow process of rekindling his fire. He was approaching it from a very different personal place.

The band's social life can be traced through their first four albums. Where *Definitely Maybe* had been the sound of a band looking for a way out of the boredom of everyday existence *What's The Story...* was the sound of the party really getting started. Confident, welcoming, the groove had been found. *Be Here Now*, with its over-zealous and crowded production mirrored the kind of party you wished you could leave if only you could face going home.

Standing on the Shoulder of Giants, then, was the crash that was almost inevitably going to follow that hedonistic ascendancy. It was less a night on the town than a meeting at a rehab clinic. It is no coincidence that the title *Where Did it All Go Wrong?* had previously been considered for the album. However, at the stage Gallagher first considered the early title he had done so ironically. As he adjusted to a slower pace of life he was indeed in a more reflective mood. There was plenty to reflect on, too. By the time the album was released, Gallagher's band had lost two of its members.

The two founding members departed in as many weeks in the summer of 1999. First to leave was guitarist Arthurs. He explained that, while recording in France, he felt that for him there was something lacking from the overall experience. 'The original spark didn't feel like it was there, it really didn't,' he said. 'I don't know it had just gone.' He said he had mulled the idea of going through the motions, but feared that he would in truth be giving it less than he knew he should. 'I just thought I can't go on with this, to sort of kid people I'm giving my all when I won't be so I just made my decision, that was the main reason,' he said, looking back. Bonehead had always been something of a cult figure within the band. While his guitar technique had never been dazzling, he would be missed by the band's diehard fans.

Next to leave was Paul McGuigan. A statement issued by the band's label announced: 'Paul has finished his work on the recordings of the new album and feels now is an opportune time to leave before the band undertakes touring and promotional activities later on this year.' Guigsy had previously, and temporarily, left the band in 1995, when he was suffering from exhaustion. A statement made by Noel at that time added extra weight to the uncertainty that would greet his permanent departure, four years later. 'Paul is Oasis – if he leaves the band is finished,' Noel had said in 1995. 'It is that simple.'

The Gallagher brothers discussed the departure of their two band mates in August 1999, at a downbeat press conference. Both wore sunglasses, despite it being held indoors. Where that might have smacked of rock star cool three years earlier, their shades now leant them a funereal look. The band's drummer, White, was not present. Noel Gallagher began by saying, 'They've both got kids and there's no point in us kicking the doors in and saying, "Come on, we're going on tour." You've got to respect their decision. They are family men; it could be us one day.' However, looking to the future, Gallagher was far from his usual defiant self. 'We're left holding the shit sandwich,' he said. His brother was defiantly upbeat but Gallagher seemed increasingly glum as the press conference continued. His usual witty way with the media was absent. 'There might not be a stampede to join the band anyway, we've got a bit of a bad reputation,' he said. In any case, he added, the remaining members of Oasis were not 'going to rush' the search for replacements. 'We don't want to pick the first two people that come along. It's difficult, because we just don't want to drag session musicians in, because it would look stupid.'

Nobody would have suggested that the two original members had contributed a massive amount in purely musical terms. But this wasn't the point. Not only had the cycle which culminated in *Be Her Now* ended, but the gang ethos which had been such an important part of the band was eroding. The fig leaf that it wasn't all the brothers and, specifically, Noel Gallagher, was harder to keep in place. The gloomy attitude of the normally chipper Noel at the press conference did little to dampen speculation that the band were, in fact, on the brink of permanent collapse. One journalist present commented that they looked like the stuffing had been knocked out of them. As always happened whenever they had a bad tour or the Gallaghers had a bust-up, music and news websites opened polls and discussions over whether Oasis had a future. Old time music critic Nick Kent claimed that, whatever the answer to that question, 'something important has undoubtedly died' in the camp. All the while, Gallagher's previous statement that, without Guigsy, the band would be 'finished' might well have been echoing uncomfortably in his head. It had been the bassist's departure that had hit Noel hardest. Of Arthurs' exit, Noel had merely sniffed: 'Well, it's hardly Paul McCartney leaving the Beatles, is it?'

The cloud of uncharacteristic self-doubt seemed to hover. It was discernible in the sound of band's fourth album; for some listeners a good thing. That said, its bombastic opener, 'Fucking in the Bushes', scarcely lacked energy or belief. The more surprising element was that Gallagher was showing Oasis fans the fruits of his explorations into new territory. This was almost a dancefloor track – certainly as close as the band had ever come to such a beast. More familiar service was resumed with 'Go Let it Out', a melodic, textbook Beatles-like Gallagher tune. As one reviewer noted, it was as if Paul Weller had left the studio long enough for the band to muck about with track one, but he had returned in time for them to immediately revert to type for its successor. In any case, Gallagher then rated 'Go Let it Out' as 'up there with some of the best things that I've done'.

It was with track three that the more introspective Gallagher coyly began to show its face. Amid his newfound clarity he had written the song for wife Meg Mathews called 'Who Feels Love?' which, as recorded, would be a single dripping with the far-out, hippy vibe that drenched the album. It had been influenced by a trip to Thailand, during which he and Mathews visited a temple. 'It was the calm after the storm,' he said. 'I suppose I was feeling at one with the world.' At the opposite end of the spectrum was

'Gas Panic!', the track inspired by his own night terrors. 'I like it because it's dark,' he said. 'It's a catchy little number without being pop.'

The two tracks sung by Noel were full of unaccustomed regret. 'Where Did It All Go Wrong?', the initial title for the album, brought up questions of age and wondering about keeping receipts for the friends he had bought. The dark feeling poured into the next song, 'Sunday Morning Call'. Again, Noel was on vocals and again, the sense of a genuinely dark morning after is to the fore. Here, he was admonishing another feckless character, whose lifestyle has left them alone and hearing voices in the darkness. Speculation over the subject of the track soon began and he would himself later describe these two songs as 'the most factually correct on the record, because they're about certain real people who I know, but who, obviously, remain nameless.' Gallagher seemed to be processing his own fast life over the previous few years and wondering just who it was he had let in so close to him.

The sort of caricatures he painted of them is familiar enough. 'People who used to always turn up on my fucking doorstep but at ungodly hours of the morning – and these are proper, well-off, rich, famous people, quite young. And they'd be running you through their drug and booze hell and they ultimately think that to sort all this out they just write a cheque made payable to the Priory clinic and six weeks later everyone's going to come up smelling of roses.' Dripping with cynicism over the increasing collision of the celebrity and rehab worlds, he pointed out that six weeks later the same people would be crying in his kitchen again.

Gallagher's working-class Manchester childhood would return to him at such moments. He would remind the tearful petals, 'At least you're not washing car windscreens for a living on fucking Baker Street. Get a grip of yourself, man.' He was all for people stepping off the narcotic conveyor belt but he felt that the cheque book was the wrong way to do so. 'It's like, if you don't want to do it no more, then don't do it,' he said. 'But for fuck's sake don't spend 20 grand trying to kick the habit that you can just kick by looking in the mirror and saying to yourself, "Where did all this go wrong, man?" That's basically what them songs are about. I suppose they're subconsciously directed at myself in some ways.'

The album was also significant in that it included the first song written by his brother. Indeed, this was the first Oasis to be written by anyone other than Noel Gallagher. The result, 'Little James', was primitive and uncertain and has been much derided. But it was an important line that had been crossed in the band. Even in relinquishing control to the extent that another song writer chipped in, Noel was careful to point out he was fully behind its inclusion. 'It's a good song,' he said. 'I wouldn't have let it be on the album otherwise.'

For all its positives, *Standing...* was an album not devoid of turkeys. 'Put Yer Money Where Your Mouth Is' was unimaginative, uninspiring and forgettable. 'I Can See a Liar' was also not much more than the sum of its fine vocals. The album's finale, 'Roll it Over', was a bit of work short of a classic Gallagher flag waver. Again, Gallagher's discomfort at his life in recent years surfaced with pointed references to those fair weather friends who would eat at his table without bringing anything to it. Any of these people who heard these lyrics, a procession of liggers and hangers-on who had gleefully partied with him for years, might have shuffled uncomfortably at the undoubted truth they conveyed. However, this was no 'Champagne Supernova' – it was at best a Cava Supernova.

From the beginning of the process of putting together the album, Gallagher had been keen to take more risks. 'I decided that I wasn't going to use anything that I'd used on any of the previous three albums,' he said. 'I put away all the guitars and Marshall stacks I'd used on ...*Morning Glory*, *Be Here Now* and *Definitely Maybe*. Then I bought loads of really weird pedals, old guitars, and small amps.' His willingness to experiment owed as much as anything to a lack of tight deadline for the album. This made him more inclined to try new instruments, effects and styles. It also gave him more time to do that thing he rarely liked to admit to: put in the hours. 'I worked harder on that album than anything before and anything since,' he said.

In more recent times he has distanced himself from this fourth studio effort. In fact, he could hardly have been more damningly exact: 'We should have never made *Standing on the Shoulder of Giants*,' he later said. 'I'd come to the end. At the time, I had no reason or desire to make music. I had no drive. We'd sold all these fucking records and there just seemed to be no point.' Indeed, it was his brother who was the driving force behind the album. Noel reported he had said the impetus to get back in the studio when they did was his. While Noel felt more inclined to hire a boat 'and sail around the Bahamas or whatever', he nonetheless didn't seem to be able to come up with any more reasons for not agreeing to get on with more work. 'I just wrote songs for the sake of making an album.'

He was in a period of transition not only as a man but as a songwriter too. He had left behind the worst excesses – both musical and celebratory – of the 1990s, but had yet to rediscover his confidence in and out of the music industry. While relentlessly proud, almost boastful, of the fact he kicked drugs without entering a rehab clinic, he did seek and receive help. 'I was off drugs, but to get off those I had to go on prescription drugs, which is fucking worse because they come from a doctor,' he said. 'It's just uppers and downers that replace the cocaine and booze.'

Standing... was a landmark if only for being the first album released through the Gallaghers' own Big Brother Recordings company. Creation Records was coming to an end, following Alan McGee's announcement in November 1999 that he was leaving the company he had started. Creation's final album was appropriately titled – or at least pronounced – *XTRMNTR*, by Primal Scream. But Creation's trajectory had always been tied to the fortunes of their biggest asset in Oasis and that band had long stopped needing either the label or McGee himself to shift records. Oasis would show that they could comfortably manage the whole process on their own.

While they would comfortably hit UK No 1 again, the critical reception to the album was mixed and for the first time in the band's existence, muted. It was the tacit recognition that they had become more of a permanent fixture on the landscape rather than the unpredictable force they'd been before. *NME* awarded it just six out of 10, the review complaining that 'very few of the greatest pop bands know when to knock it on the head' and that the album 'has a half-finished air about it'. *Rolling Stone* came to the same conclusion, giving the album three out of five. It highlighted 'Go Let it Out' as the album's highlight, saying, 'If we must endure vague platitudes shouted from the rooftop, let them all sound this gloriously drunk with belligerence.' Perhaps the best critic of *Standing...* has been the passage of time. Most of its tracks quickly disappeared from Oasis live sets, with only *Rolling Stone*'s favourite appearing on a subsequent greatest hits compilation. Gallagher has himself been disinclined to return to the album during his live sets as a solo artist. At least *Be Here Now* had been something to get passionate about, even if many critics and Gallagher himself had taken against it. *Standing...* didn't seem to make a great impact in any sense.

Yet the album did serve as a useful bridge, taking the band from the overenthusiastic noise and bombast of *Be Here Now* towards a new and more thoughtful era. Noel explained the musical intricacy behind this. 'I used to just turn up the amps as full as I could get them – I never used distortion pedals or anything like that,' he said. 'But I started collecting Ibanez Tube Screamers recently, and I've got an old '70s model, which is the best pedal I've ever come across. So now I get a really good rhythm sound, and then kick in a Tube Screamer for the guitar solos. I like that so much better than having a loud guitar sound going all the time.' He admitted that none of this constituted a 'radical change from the past', but the sense that a corner was being turned did remain. The innovations had given Gallagher confidence to introduce more of them. 'At least,' he said, 'I know that I can combine rock'n'roll with a contemporary feel and that gives me the confidence to go on.'

He would also be going with a band containing two new members, as the search for Guigsy and Bonehead's replacements was swiftly completed. It was only shortly after *Standing...* had been recorded that the new Oasis line-up was finalised. The easiest decision had been to replace Arthurs with Heavy Stereo main man Gem Archer. Gallagher had been friends with Archer for a while, Heavy Stereo having supported Oasis at Knebworth and Loch Lomand. Like the two Gallagher brothers, Heavy Stereo were also contributing a track to the Jam tribute album *Fire & Skill* which was to come out that November. It had mixed reviews but showed the shared influences were impeccable. Archer's passion for music was impressive and made the choice a breeze.

'I just phoned him up,' Gallagher said. 'And we didn't even bother... doing the audition thing because we were fans of

Heavy Stereo anyway and so we knew he could play. So that was that sort of boxed off within a matter of days.'

Filling the bassist vacancy was a lengthier and more considered process. Gallagher has since spoken of several months of auditions with a number of bassists, some of whom were currently in big name bands. 'They sort of came down on the sly, under the cover of darkness,' he said, adding that it was like being on *Stars in their Eyes* for a few months. Eventually, they settled on Andy Bell, whose band Ride had been effectively sidelined by the arrival of Oasis at Creation. It was nothing personal – everyone was sidelined when Gallagher's outfit turned up – but then there was Hurricane #1, often mocked, and not least by the Gallaghers. Bell had once made some derogatory comments about Liam. In revenge, Noel had once remarked: 'I see Hurricane #1 went in at Number 35. That's 35 places too high in my book.' A spell with music journalist Cliff Jones' Gay Dad did little to enhance his credibility but despite any previous disagreements, Gallagher was never one to overlook talent.

Bell also provided something of a middle class dimension to the band. A well-spoken man from Oxford, this was in itself a marked contrast with the previous Oasis members. Gallagher would sometimes mock Bell's accent during interviews and concerts and even encouraged the audience to chant, 'Who the fuck is Andy Bell?' at one performance. Perhaps nobody was more surprised than Gallagher that Bell turned up for the job. 'I was amazed that Andy was up for actually playing the bass y'know, 'cos he's such a good guitarist,' he said. Bell had never played bass before but reasoned that Gallagher had made him 'an offer I couldn't refuse'. Apart from anything else, Both new members had fine, Gallagher-esque hairstyles but more usefully shook up Oasis, just when the band most needed that to happen.

Talking to *Hot Press*, Gallagher sounded more relaxed about what the future held. 'The beauty of all this is that I haven't got a fucking clue what the next Oasis album will sound like. If Andy has anything to do with it, it's going to sound like the Rolling Stones. If Gem's got anything to do with it, it's going to sound like the Faces. And if I've got anything to do with it, it'll sound like all those fucking bands plus my own thing.'

Meg Mathews marked the couple's second wedding anniversary by announcing she was pregnant. This created a further welcome chance for the future father to slow down. 'I like that I'm not going to be able to let myself go any more, because I'm going to have to be there,' he said. 'Meg always wanted kids, anyway, and I was, like, well, if it happens it happens, but I was over the moon that it did.' He decided he wanted the baby to be a girl. He had two brothers and was in a band with 'five geezers': there were enough men in his life.

On 27 January 2000, Mathews did indeed give birth to a baby daughter. She was born early in the afternoon at the Portland hospital and Noel was present. Alongside him were his mother Peggy and Meg's mother Chris. Months before the birth, Noel had confessed that he had conjured a nightmarish vision of it in his head. 'I've got a mental picture of the birth like some scene from *The Exorcist*, with loads of swearing, people in masks, screaming, shouting, a smoke machine,' he said, adding he had 'felt like an idiot standing there' at the birth. Typical diversionary humour from him, but during the birth he had been so moved that he burst into tears.

They named the girl Anaïs, after the French author Anaïs Nin. He was photographed celebrating the birth near the hospital with a pint of Guinness and a cigarette, looking most accomplished. He was quickly joined by a gaggle of reporters. He explained why he had left the hospital. 'They were all drinking champagne and I don't like champagne, so I came in here,' he said. Just four months earlier, Liam had also become a father when his wife Patsy Kensit gave birth to Lennon Francis. Peggy was, Noel said, delighted. 'It's like a bus: you wait ten years for a grandchild then two come along at once.'

For any man, becoming a father is an obvious landmark and life-changer. For Noel and Liam, having had such a disrupted home life themselves as kids, the significance was greater. Much research has been done into the supposed cycle of poor parenting and how it gets passed down through the generations. The theory is that those who have been treated badly or abused may go on to do the same things themselves, perhaps as a subconscious way of retaining a measure of the control they didn't have when they were younger.

Despite the fame that had brought Noel Gallagher the riches to be able to leave the material poverty of his childhood far behind, the challenges of bringing up a child remained. This wasn't something you could buy and even the most well-adjusted child will have a lot to deal with when they get to adulthood and have to take on the responsibility themselves. Looking back 12 years later, on those first months of fatherhood Gallagher said, 'I didn't have the tools instinctively.' However, he was keen to learn, commenting in 2001 that, 'for the child that I have and the children that I hope to have, I want to be a good and approachable father.'

But Gallagher had been building a new kind of stability in his life long before fatherhood. He had worked to separate his personal and professional lives, even creating a physical divide that mirrored the mental one in his mind. 'Outside my home is bullshit, inside is calm,' he said. Giving an insight into life as one of the country's most famous musicians, he explained how any trip out in London became like part of the job the moment he left the car that had driven him there. 'You take a deep breath at the door and as soon as you open the door, you're on duty and it's as simple as that. It's like you're clocking in.' He said how if he went to a concert, most people would want a photograph or an autograph – the rest would want to mock him. As a result, he simply made fewer trips into London. To a large extent he had, anyway, stepped off the celebrity treadmill – a place he had never been entirely comfortable. 'My life revolves around proper things like family and friends,' he said. 'I can actually walk round the garden without somebody sticking a camera up my arse'. It was typically light. Gallagher was always essentially comfortable with the attention that the press heaped on him.

Now he was living in the Buckinghamshire countryside just beyond the M25. It was quieter, but that was what he wanted. He would only later move back to London to settle not far from Belsize Park in Maida Vale years later. Every inch the rock star, he nevertheless didn't let it get in the way of living. 'Life is a great thing, why shut yourself away from it? I can't understand people like Elton John and Robbie Williams going straight from their blacked-out limos to a restaurant. I stand in the queue at Waitrose. More rock stars should do that. Forget therapy, go to the supermarket and interact. The staff in my local Waitrose are really blasé about me now. They'll be like, "Him? Oh he's in here all the fucking time. And between me and you, he doesn't eat very well".'

For now, getting away from urban life suited him. Once, he said, he would have thought, 'Thou shalt act like a rock star. But now I like getting bored.' Yet, when excitement came, it wasn't the kind that he would have welcomed even in the maddest moments back in the Supernova Heights days. It wasn't long after the stabbing and wounding of George Harrison at his country house in December 1999 that Gallagher returned home to find someone he had never met quietly sitting at the table in the kitchen. The man had just broken into the house, having heard that Gallagher had moved to the area and was waiting for him as if it was perfectly normal. Gallagher and a friend kept him talking over a cup of tea while Mathews called the police. The intruder tried to make a run for it but was caught without any injury to Gallagher.

When some harm was done, it was between the two brothers as the two fell out during the Standing on the Shoulder of Giants tour. Nothing new in a Gallagher row and indeed there wasn't. But this was the beginning of a fundamental shift in the relationship between the two – commentators would later trace back the final falling out to the ructions of 2000, though it would take almost nine years for the process.

The tour had begun at the end of February in Japan and by 20 May the band were back in Europe, in Barcelona and in good shape, apart from drummer White, who had damaged his wrist and was unable to play. In the enforced downtime that evening, one of the biggest rows between the Gallaghers to date broke out after Liam got very personal with his brother. Noel later said, 'I lost it with him. It was a proper fight – it wasn't just like, "I'll scratch your eyes out, you bitch!" It was a proper brawl and I'm actually quite proud of the fact that it came to blows. He knows that if he crosses me that far I'll leave him in the shit.' And he did, walking off the tour and although, after Mother Earth guitarist Matt Deighton substituted for a number of dates, he subsequently returned, there was undeniably something that had changed – this was the row that they kept coming back to. Later asked by the *NME* if he ever apologised for his part in whatever had happened, Liam didn't answer directly but passed the question to his brother.

'I think you may have,' said Noel, 'in your own little way. You certainly didn't say the word "Sorry".'

Meanwhile, as he left the tour, Noel announced that his days of touring outside of the UK with the band were over. The warning was taken seriously. Indeed, given that Noel had recently told *Time Out*, 'Watching my little girl grow up is far more important than watching the band develop', there were fears that he might go one stage further and quit the band altogether. 'We don't have a relationship outside the band. We are not good at playing happy families,' said Noel of Liam.

Yet the older Gallagher returned to the live fold for the concert in Bolton. The pair shook hands and peace seemed to have returned. Then came Wembley. The band were booked to perform on two consecutive nights at the venerable stadium, their first and last appearances at the old stadium before it was demolished and rebuilt. Both nights were filmed and the first – later released as a live DVD and album, entitled *Familiar To Millions* – went without incident. However, Liam was not in a good state by the time he took the stage for the second round. 'If you think I'm over the moon to be here you're fucking tripping,' he told them. 'The songs were punctuated by mid-song ranting from Liam.

Oasis concerts had never been polished affairs, but this relentless clowning seemed to be enraging Noel.

The audience, however, were loving it. The tension between the Gallaghers had afforded the usually impersonal stadium the intimacy of a pub concert. Which Oasis fan did not adore the long-running and legendary tension between the brothers Gallagher? Noel had moments of sweet victory as the evening wore on. As Liam returned to the stage after one of the songs sung by Noel, he asked the audience: 'Shall we let Noel carry on?' The audience roared its approval for the idea. 'You fucking cheeky bunch of bastards!' replied Liam, as Noel enjoyed the moment. Whatever emotions he might have been feeling he seemed to be fully in control of and he engaged in banter with his brother where he could.

It wasn't just the brotherly relationship which was under pressure. Noel's marriage had not lasted through his transition to a different mode of life. By the beginning of 2001, Gallagher and Mathews had split. The divorce was confirmed in the third week of January. Mathews had filed for divorce on the grounds of alleged adultery by Gallagher with his new partner, Sara McDonald. And as with fatherhood so with divorce: Liam had split from Patsy Kensit the previous year, pipping his elder brother to this rather less welcome milestone. Professionally and personally: wherever you looked in the early years of the new millennium, life seemed increasingly uncertain for Noel Gallagher.

The most significant professional uncertainty was about to show itself. Within Oasis, there had previously been two camps: the Gallaghers and the remainder of the band. For all their famed rivalry, the brothers had always had a bond that the other members could not puncture. Now, however, there was a growing shift in the dynamics, one that would leave Noel increasingly isolated.

CHAPTER 10

FORCE OF NATURE

'IF YOU LOOK AT MATTERS CAREFULLY YOU WILL SEE
THAT SOMETHING RESEMBLING VIRTUE, IF YOU FOLLOW
IT, MAY BE YOUR RUIN, WHILE SOMETHING ELSE
RESEMBLING VICE WILL LEAD, IF YOU FOLLOW
IT, TO YOUR SECURITY AND WELL BEING.'
NICCOLO MACHIAVELLI (*THE PRINCE*, 1532)

Noel Gallagher was ever more frequently offered guest slots on stage alongside other artists he admired. He could be relied upon to add musical chops without being flashy and the aura of naughtiness which hung around Oasis gave a shot to the rock'n'roll reputations of the more established acts he played with.

As well as regularly popping up with the likes of Paul Weller and various Brit Pop era ensembles such as Ocean Colour Scene, he was called on for important charity and tribute gigs. In April 2001 there was a concert celebrating the life of Small Faces frontman Steve Marriott. The bill included Humble Pie and even Midge Ure. But it was the climax of the evening in which Gallagher was in his element, appearing alongside Paul Weller, Alan White, Gem Archer and Small Faces members, organist Ian McLagan and drummer Kenney Jones, for an encore that was greeted with deafening acclaim. They performed five songs, including ode to speed 'Here Comes the Nice' on which Gallagher took lead vocals. As the night reached its crescendo with a chaotic, ensemble performance of the anthemic 'All Or Nothing', both Gallagher and Weller were openly delirious with joy. Here, the acclaim and success they had both amassed in their own careers seemed to fall away and they both looked like they had become boys again, unable to believe their luck that they were playing on-stage in a 21st century representation of the Small Faces.

Away from this concert there had rarely been any doubt about who was the senior figure in the relationship, and not just in terms of age. Gallagher, who over the years has guest performed at numerous Weller concerts, was once asked how he felt about the fact that Weller rarely returned the compliment by joining Oasis on stage. At the time, Gallagher shrugged off the awkward moment with a joke, pretending he heckled Weller from the side of the stage. But he simply had a long way to go before he could emulate Weller's success with the Jam, Style Council and as a solo artist, in a career that lasted the best part of five decades. It was a longevity and scale of influence that

Gallagher could aspire to and no amount of defensive quips could disguise it.

The Marriott memorial was not the only time that Gallagher performed with rock legends in London in the early years of the century. The Who performed a concert at the Royal Albert Hall for the Teenage Cancer Trust. Gallagher joined them on-stage for their 'Won't Get Fooled Again'. Gallagher's evident delight as the song reached its power chord highs was touching. (Weller, too, had joined the band to sing 'So Sad about Us'. The terrifying yellow jumper he sported showed that even a style guru can have an off day.) The Who slot was another reminder of how Gallagher now had the ermine robes and permanent seat in rock's upper house, though he was always first to laugh off the accolades with self-deprecatory stories. He told one music journalist of how he had difficulties with his visa in entering the US and was one of those unlucky enough to be pulled aside for a lengthy interrogation by the ever-diligent employees of the US immigration service. He explained that just a few months later he was once more taken aside – though this encounter was not as drawn out. 'Some guy looks at his screen and calls someone else over,' Gallagher told the paper. By the sound of the official's good-old-boy voice and the ease with which he wore sizeable gun he looked to be a citizen of the Deep South. Not, in other words, someone that Gallagher might have relished having a one-on-one with. 'After a few minutes he says, "Can you answer a question

for me, sir?" He's holding this massive gun and he goes...
"What was it like when y'all met Pete Townshend?"'

Meanwhile, the evolution of Oasis continued apace, as the
band's two new members found their places and, most
pertinently, songwriting voices in the line-up. As Archer
explained, with Gallagher having written some of the finest
tracks of the age, it took confidence for him and Bell to raise
their hands and suggest a new track. But he was more
encouraging than he had been before of soliciting new
material and they were more accomplished musicians than
the original members had been. Suddenly, Oasis included
four song-writers. 'Before,' said Gallagher, creating an
imaginary scenario, 'if someone walked into the room and
asked: "Who is the songwriter?" I would jump up and say,
"That would be me." Now, though, half the bloody room
stands up!' It was a new feeling, but he was saying this with
some enthusiasm. Elsewhere, he proudly described the Oasis
as 'a jet with four engines instead of one.'

At the heart of the band, the brothers were back on
working terms as they went into start on the first album to
feel the benefit of quadruple engine power, *Heathen
Chemistry*. This was the first time they were to do sustained
work as new fathers and while they exuded as much energy
as ever, both were now mostly enjoying a far less extreme
version of the rock'n'roll lifestyle. There was in every way a
new beginning for the band. That said, questions were still
regularly asked of Noel about his personal life. The press
were particularly relentless in their interest in Gallagher's

split. 'I get unfairly singled out about marriage,' he said to Q
a year later, dropping in a customary dig at Radiohead for
good measure. 'No one asks Thom Yorke about his
marriage.' He wouldn't be drawn on the causes of the end
of the marriage. 'I haven't got any bad blood towards my ex
... It's just it got to the point where there was nothing more
for me to say to her, nothing more for her to say to me, so
I said, "I'm off." We only speak when it's to do with Anaïs.
That's it. Other than that, it's gone.' He would look after her
each week for a regular period, generally seeing his daughter
on a Thursday or a Friday. 'She draws all over my face,' he
said. He pointed out that while his relationship with his ex-
wife had simply not survived his move to the countryside,
Oasis was flourishing for exactly the same reason.

'Two years ago, maybe the band wasn't that important, but
the reason the band's stayed together is 'cos it has to, because
basically I've got fuck all else to be going on with in my life,'
he said, going on to qualify this dramatic statement slightly,
'apart from the group – and me little daughter and me
girlfriend and that pretty much rounds it all off for me.' This
sounded very much like someone who realised that work
and family was all he really needed and it seemed that he
was not in the least missing the woozy days of Supernova
Heights. When it came down to it, Gallagher's instinct for
what worked and what he needed to do was razor sharp.
When he needed to, he could simply move on with
apparently little anguish.

The first hints of the new album's material were

showcased during the anniversary tour of the autumn of 2001. It seemed extraordinary but no fewer than ten years had passed since Oasis played their first show at the Manchester Boardwalk and they were still doing it, still holding it together. Few would have put money on that particular anniversary at almost any point in the previous decade and it was a measure of Gallagher's determination and resolve that it had rolled around with everything still more or less in place.

The tickets for the small tour had gone on sale on 18 August and the series of smaller venues than usual inevitably sold out immediately. The celebration, named Ten Years of Noise and Confusion, started in October with gigs at London's Shepherd's Bush Empire. 'There's no significance to it, other than the fact that we're celebrating,' Gallagher told *NME*. 'We're our own biggest fans anyway and we're going on the road to celebrate that we're fucking mega.' Many of the fans who had grabbed the tickets had grown up with the band too. Apart from the millions in the bank and the adulation, they were going through the same stuff – relationships that hadn't worked out, settling into a career, having kids. The Brit Pop kids were heading inexorably towards their 30s, though Gallagher senior was relieved when he attended a Razorlight concert and found the audience – who looked to him like 'a youth club' – approaching him to tell him how the Oasis debut album had 'changed their lives'. His influence was still there, but there was no hiding from his advancing years.

As one of the Shepherds Bush Empire gigs began, news channels were announcing the start of the allied bombing of Afghanistan, following the attacks on the World Trade Center by Bin Laden. This gave the evening a strange atmosphere. The younger Gallagher milked it to great effect by appearing onstage in a camouflage jacket, and declaring: 'It's fookin' war, man.' The atmosphere went up another gear when Paul Weller, finally returning the compliment, arrived on-stage to join the band in a 'Champagne Supernova'.

Music in the UK was going through its own upheavals and evolution. Gallagher had been around long enough to see how music was going and like every generation looking back at the newest kids on the block he didn't approve of what he saw. 'Alternative music is now like fucking Val Doonican to me, the same with football. The last two, great working class things, football and music, they're coaching all the talent out of people – we will sign you up and we will culture all the talent out of you. Music should be spontaneous! And football. And all the arts. I just find it really sinister.' It wasn't just the suits of the industry that he blamed, but bands themselves as well. It could be said that the accusation that bands were only out to make as much as they could in the short term was one that had been levelled as his band in their time, but it was certainly true that Gallagher wasn't the only one to have noticed how Brit Pop had given way to the 21st century phenomenon described as 'indie landfill' who rotated around the big venues and festival circuits each year, interchangeably providing reliable entertainment for those who could afford the increasing prices of a weekend's stay in a field.

Ever the contrarian, though, he singled out a surprising candidate for his band of the moment. 'To me,' he told *City Life*, 'the best band out there is Coldplay but we're not really in competition with them. Chris Martin is a fucking genius as far as I'm concerned.' And yet they were not that different. After all, Coldplay had taken that recipe for the arms-in-air anthem to the next level. Like Oasis, their music virtually demanded to be heard in a large field with thousands of enthusiastic fans who knew every word. This was the real lesson that had been waiting to be learned from Radiohead, if only Liam had been able to do the falsetto bit. Someone who knew music as well as Gallagher was never going to go only for bands who sounded as raw as his could. Coldplay had gone the smart route. In the same interview of 2004 he said, 'But all in all, this has been a fucking disappointing year for bands' second albums.'

As far as he was concerned, most of the bands of the moment were 'top live but the music's shit.' As for the likes of Razorlight and Peter Doherty of Babyshambles, Gallagher felt they were able to produce an era-defining work that would take the mantle from Oasis, but wondered if they lacked the focus to realise their own potential. But if nothing else the lack of any clear rival meant that he could hold onto the top spot in that weird no man's land between the last gasps of credible indie and mainstream acceptance.

But even so, it wouldn't come without effort and

Gallagher was determined his band should return to form. The result was *Heathen Chemistry*. Its opener, 'The Hindu Times', was a more up-tempo affair compared with the version the band had occasionally played live prior to the album's completion. Its straightforward positivity marked the end of the cloud that had gathered over much of their previous two studio works, though it would mark their last UK No 1 single for three years. Gallagher's first lead vocals of the album arrived in the shape of 'Force of Nature', a rather plodding track. But if it chugged along like the old Oasis that was no surprise – it was, having been held over from the ...*Shoulder* sessions. It had been written in 1998 and on Jude Law's request it was recorded for gangster film *Love, Honour and Obey*, released in 2000.

'Force of Nature' featured another example of lyrics targeted at those who had done Gallagher wrong and there were suggestions that it was aimed at his ex-wife. He denied those interpretations and said that he deliberately held back from including songs about his own relationships. When he did, in songs such as the gossamer light 'She is Love', he said it was in a more general sense about his own happiness. He was content with Sara MacDonald and the lyric reflected the equal playing field they operated on. 'I don't', he reminded the *Sunday Telegraph*, 'like to write achingly personal songs.' He remained instead drawn to the generalised notions of happiness and contentment. The lyrics drew on Khalil Gibran, the early 20th century Lebanese author of *The Prophet*, who wrote 'On Love': 'And with a great voice he said:/When love beckons to you follow him/Though his ways are hard and steep.' Gibran had also been a source of inspiration for the Beatles, as Gallagher may have known, with 'Julia' from the *White Album* having also adapted lines from Gibran.

Following Archer's glam-rockish 'Hung in a Bad Place' comes one of the album's two highlights, 'Stop Crying Your Heart Out'. Although Gallagher had long stopped defining his times, this track had elements of what had made his work iconic. *Heathen...*'s other highlight is 'Little By Little', another sung by Gallagher, which became a staple of the live sets of Oasis and later Gallagher's solo shows. This was the clearest signpost to how he would sound on his own – his voice was a direct blast, more powerful than ever before, despite the lyrics being as chock full of abstractly reassuring statements of community as ever. A video featured actor Robert Carlyle in diminutive form and Gallagher as confident as he had ever looked.

By contrast, the songs written by the other three jet engines were never going to threaten Gallagher's position as the band's song writing centre. As well as 'Hung in a Bad Place', there was an entirely forgettable short instrumental from Bell and 'Songbird' from Liam. This was quite the step forward from the younger Gallagher's previous efforts and showed how it wasn't just Noel who was beginning to develop independently. '"Songbird" blew my fucking head off when I first heard it,' he commented, 'because it's that fucking simple'. The album sold well enough to reach UK

No 1 – where it went triple platinum – and to reach the top
ten of several other European countries.

Critical opinion was far more mixed. The *NME's*
measured view was, 'the days when you took the country's
pulse from their albums have long gone, but play it loud and
you can still believe this is the band who hosted the biggest
rock'n'roll block party since punk.' *Rolling Stone*, though,
believed that, 'As the principal songwriter of Oasis, Noel
Gallagher may have gone as far as he can with the pop song'
and argued that '"Little by Little" is the kind of earnest ...
crap even Bryan Adams would know to edit.' The *Guardian*
suggested that the album signalled the end of the band,
saying: 'There is a finality about *Heathen Chemistry*, the
band's third hopeless attempt in a row.' The same reviewer
took aim at Gallagher personally, writing, 'As a lyricist,
Gallagher has always been more David Coleman than David
Bowie, frequently giving the impression that English is his
second language.'

Chiding Noel Gallagher for a lack of lyrical clarity
seemed to be a pursuit that verged on the heartless and
certainly was entirely pointless. It was as if the press had
never quite forgiven the Oasis camp for their own
embarrassingly fulsome reception of *Be Here Now* and kept
wanting to revisit that particular open sore. If anything,
the fact that Oasis were not merely still existing but
producing records that sold in their millions – *Heathen
Chemistry* managed around a million at home – was more
astonishing in the 21st century than some of their fresher

accomplishments when they started out. By now Gallagher was more relaxed as a creative force. That he still had the drive to produce new music showed how much it meant to him, when he could have just gone into rock star salmon-farming retirement. The furthest he seemed to want to go was to allow the others a go at the writing side of things.

It had been one of the first instructions that Gallagher had said to his new recruits. ''Cos I'm kind of done,' he explained. 'I wasn't done with writing songs, but done with kind of driving it on my own.' Yet he offered no special favours. Anyone in the band who wanted to contribute a song had to work it up to final form and to be willing to produce it themselves. By now the new arrivals had seen the finishing touches put to ...*Shoulder* and had a chance to decide on their creative approach. That didn't make it any easier, looking at the boots they had to fill, of whose size their owner was certainly keenly – and amusedly – aware.

'I think at first attempt they both tried to write what they thought were Oasis songs. I remember just saying to them, "Look, just write songs. Don't write about what you think Oasis should like, 'cos that's just fucking ridiculous." And once we had that conversation it was fine.' The creative reservoir was once again topped up – more, in fact. 'So now we've got loads of songs all the time ... somebody has to choose or they'd constantly be triple albums coming out.' This was a refreshed-sounding Noel Gallagher in conversation. They still had a few No 1 songs in them yet and they could come from more angles than before, though as Gallagher memorably said to Q, 'The old mongrel always gets his nose in the bowl first,' when it came to selecting songs for release.

With 'Little by Little' and 'Hindu Times' mentioning God, curiosity over whether Gallagher held religious or spiritual beliefs was rekindled. He always shrugged the question off by simply stating that the concept of god makes for good lyrical imagery. The Irish Catholic hangover had not been as big for him as it was for many others. But given the intensity with which many of his songs have been received, Gallagher had grown accustomed to listeners reading what they want to into the tracks. One man approached him to tell him how much ...*Morning Glory*'s 'Some Might Say' meant to him due to his Christianity. This had taken place long before Gallagher gave up his partying ways and he had been, by his own admission, 'drugged up to the eyeballs' as this conversation took place.

In August, Gallagher almost had cause to revisit his casual attitude to the afterlife when he experienced a moment of very mortal fear after being hospitalised following a car crash in America. Alongside Andy Bell and keyboard player Jay Darlington, he was injured when the car they were travelling in collided with another vehicle in downtown Indianapolis. Liam was not involved. He had, in fact, just weeks earlier faced a drama himself when his voice failed during a concert in Fort Lauderdale, Florida, forcing him to retire from the performance just four songs in. Once again, an Oasis tour in America was being hit by hitches, but compared to the seismic ructions of their early tours in the 1990s it was all fairly minor stuff.

Gallagher's true religion remained Manchester City and one of the things that made him proudest was learning that Manchester City fans had adapted 'Wonderwall' to praise Georgi Kinkladze in the mid-1990s. It was a link between his twin passions that continued when Portugal defeated England in Euro 2004 on Thursday 24 June. The nation's previous international tournament exit – from the 2002 World Cup – had been defined by a Gallagher song, after the BBC played 'Stop Crying your Heart Out' during the closing credits of its coverage. In 2004, the night Oasis after the England defeat, Oasis put in a performance themselves at Glastonbury. But the verdicts were not favourable and the critics included the festival's founder. 'I'm more of an Oasis fan than a Beatles fan,' said Michael Eavis, 'but in the end Paul McCartney came over as stronger by far.' The comparison wasn't entirely fair – Sir Paul was aided by having fireworks over the iconic pyramid stage to 'Live and Let Die' and a peerless back catalogue which ensured every campfire throughout the site resounded to drunken singalongs of 'Hey Jude' for the rest of the weekend. Even top form Oasis could hardly have competed with a genuine Beatle, but there still seemed to be an element of revisionism among those who were critical of the band these days. John Harris, 1990s rock journo and author of

Brit Pop history *The Last Party*, wrote openly about how he regretted going along with Gallagher's comparisons to the Fab Four. 'It was a seductive idea,' he admitted to fellow *Guardian* writer Alexis Petridis. 'I thought that myself at the height of Brit Pop, but in the cold light of day it was an absolutely hysterical point of view, there was no excuse for it at all.'

And yet, as Danny Ecclestone of *Mojo* said at the same time, there was another way of looking at it. 'Their apogee was comparable to that of the Beatles and the Stones. There are an awful lot of people who came into loving music through liking Oasis and no amount of bad records will take that away.'

Final word on Glastonbury was delivered by Gallagher himself, who responded to the inflammatory accusation that his band had no respect for the festival's crowd in a surprising affirmative: 'We don't! We've not got respect for any crowd, not even our own.' Perhaps just another tongue in cheek Gallagher comment, there was undoubtedly an element of truth in that. Nobody who had taken the stage at a gig as big as Knebworth – twice – could really be that in awe of what the audience were expecting. Gallagher expected his audience to keep up and he was the least likely to get behind the Glastonbury ethos of love, peace and unbearable toilets with any plausibility.

Oasis was anyway no longer the sole focus of Gallagher's attention. There was the record label for one. Big Brother would issue the soundtrack to the movie *Goal!* in 2005.

Among the offerings from various artists was a new song from Gallagher with an experimental edge, 'Who Put the Weight of the World on my Shoulders?', a string-heavy song produced by UNKLE. They were also behind the similarly orchestral reworking of ...*Morning Glory*'s 'Cast No Shadow' with Noel himself on vocals this time, a more measured take than the original. Back in 2001 Gallagher had also set up his own record label, Sour Mash, which would handle other acts. If nothing else, as he said, it would 'give me something to do on my days off'. The first act to have a release were Proud Mary. Their members had been interested in replacing Guigsy and Bonehead but on hearing their tape Gallagher decided he wanted to see what they could do themselves. *The Same Old Blues* had not done particularly well but it was if nothing else an indication of the diversity of Gallagher's interests. Drummer Terry Kirkbride would maintain his connection with Gallagher, going on to provide percussion for the understated acoustic tour the pair did with Gem Archer for 2006's *Stop the Clocks*.

Don't Believe the Truth followed in 2005, a deceptively unremarkable release. This was Oasis's sixth album and while the world hadn't exactly stopped watching, it had long stopped being excited in the way that it once had. And so the revolutions that were happening were quiet ones, but fundamental for the way that Gallagher worked and the direction of the band. For one, it was around this time that he would later say he really began to be confident as a singer. Despite his creative talents and the innumerable occasions he'd performed on stage – alone or in any shape of band configuration – he'd always played the part of the guitarist augmenting his role. There was a world of difference between being able to do something and being comfortable, even enthusiastic about it. And he wasn't the only one beginning feel more comfortable in previously alien territory.

Liam – not to mention the other members of the band – had developed in their own song writing to the point where it had begun harder to see the joins with Noel's work. Indeed, of all the albums made by the second incarnation of Oasis, this was the strongest and most democratically realised. They had begun work on it at the Sawmills Studios in Cornwall, with Death In Vegas as producers. Gallagher explained humorously how he convinced his brother to accept outsiders – and not just dance influenced rockers but influential electronic artists who liked rock. 'Liam hates producers but he had worked with Death In Vegas on one of their records,' he told the *Observer*. Liam had sung on 'Scorpio Rising', from the album of the same name, some three years earlier. 'So it was like something out of *Star Wars* – we had to get Liam to think that asking them to produce the record was his idea.' However, after three weeks work, the band decided, in Gallagher's words, they 'didn't like anything' they had recorded. 'We were trying to polish a turd,' he added. But this wasn't just a production clash. They opted to start afresh, not just on recording but also in composition, going away to write new songs.

First, they had to break the news to Death in Vegas's Richard Fearless. Gallagher explained how his younger brother left the difficult duty to him. 'We called a meeting to tell him, and when he walked into the pub, Liam said: "Oh, is that my phone?" and walked off. I had to tell Richard we were going to call it a day.'

Death In Vegas didn't have more time to begin again so Gallagher was joined by American producer Dave Sardy, who had worked with a wide range of artists such as blues rock revivalists Wolfmother. He would later work on *Dig Out Your Soul* and return for Noel Gallagher's High Flying Birds. 'We'd never used a producer – ever – not until Dave,' said Gallagher. 'I know Owen Morris was credited with production but he was really an engineer and I was kind of doing it ... it was like he was in the band but he couldn't play an instrument.' Gallagher had simply realised that he didn't want to go on handling the studio work himself. They'd been recommended Sardy through his work with Australian rockers Jet, whose songs included the White Stripes-tinged rock of 'Are You Gonna be My Girl'. 'So we went to meet Dave, and we didn't really talk music. It's obvious he knows what he's fucking doing ... He's got a great sense of humour for a Yank. He liked us, we liked him...That's all there needs to be. As long as the guy behind the desk understands everybody else's personality and he's not a control freak – you know, producers running off with the tapes and all that. You can't do that with Oasis because someone will get knocked out.'

Work began at Wheeler End Studios and ended up on Sardy's home turf in California, where the album really took shape. Scorching opener 'Turn Up The Sun' was by Andy Bell. The finished version, with a heavy, glam-rock riff, was noisier and dirtier than he had intended, perhaps betraying the hand of Gallagher. 'Mucky Fingers', by contrast, was written and sung by Gallagher. Rarely had Gallagher sounded happier on record with lyrical concerns to match. On 'The Importance of Being Idle', one of three Top 3 singles from the band that year, he sounded more sedate, but blissfully so. This would be the band's last No 1 single, but they were marking their eighth in fine style. 'Like the Kinks doing the La's,' said Gallagher, 'or the La's doing the Kinks'. In production and arrangement it was the closest so far to the approach he would later adopt on *Noel Gallagher's High Flying Birds*, part trad jazz band, part supple rocker, an altogether more grown-up affair. Only on 'Part of the Queue' did he sound like the Gallagher of old. In a track with shades of the Smiths discernible, he rarely captures the imagination, Archer's comparison between the song and the Stranglers' 'Golden Brown' notwithstanding. His revelation that the song was influenced by irritatingly long queues scarcely adds to its appeal.

Perhaps the most interesting tracks came from Archer and Bell. Strong, affirmative and uplifting – Archer's 'A Bell Will Ring', a fine anthem to emotional renewal and Bell's 'Keep the Dream Alive'. As Archer commented of the track, it was the sort of song one could ride a scooter off a cliff to. If these were taken as more signposts to the future, given how Oasis would later split, this was the positivity of Beady Eye tracks against the cloudy mood of Noel at his finest on *High Flying Birds*.

At the same time, on another Gallagher track, 'Lyla', the mood, lyrics and tune could scarcely have been more festive. This became a live favourite of the album, as did 'Turn Up the Sun', which was a set opener for some time. Gallagher was impressed by the input of Bell and Archer, saying their efforts were songs he wished he had written. Gallaghers' 'Let There Be Love' was the album's triumphant conclusion. 'I'm not too sure about that one,' he later explained. 'It took me seven years to write that song. I kind of didn't want to put it on to the album as it's a ballad.' He had campaigned hard against the inclusion of any sort of 'fucking flag waver', but had ultimately accepted its place.

The incremental but important changes in the way the band worked had a noticeable effect. Critics were impressed with *Don't Believe The Truth*. *Rolling Stone*, not generally the band's best friend, declared it 'the first Oasis album in years that doesn't sound like pale self-imitation', and praised its 'increased emphasis on texture — including plenty of subdued psych-rock atmosphere'. The *Observer* gave it no less than five out of five stars, concluding: 'it makes you care about Oasis again, and makes you believe they can matter again. So our bond with them is renewed'. Both *Q* and *Spin* also awarded high scores. The overriding feeling was that Gallagher and his band were *back*.

They were also back with yet another drummer, after Alan White had been replaced by Zak Starkey, son of Beatle Ringo. One way or another, it seemed, the band were never to be free of connections with the Fab Four, though Noel hotly denied that the new drummer's parentage was the reason for his appointment. Allowing the Starr connection was 'interesting for about half an hour' and conceding the new member had anecdotes to rival his own, he added, 'I'm tired of people asking if he's only in the band just because his dad was in the Beatles. That'd be like getting Stella McCartney to do backing vocals! It'd be fucking ridiculous wouldn't it?'

As for Starkey, he lavishly praised Gallagher and the band's work rate, interviewed in a mini-documentary shot for inclusion on the CD release. 'I've never met guys like them,' said Starkey, 'they can't get in the studio fast enough'. This confirmed that, much as Gallagher brushes off suggestions he has worked at his craft, talking up in interviews how effortlessly many of his biggest hits were created and singing of the importance of being idle – he was in truth an industrious figure. Not the most rock'n'roll of attributes.

Perhaps the most revealing moment of the documentary away from Starr's contribution came at the start. Slow motion footage showed the band walking along near the studio. While Liam is seen sharing a laugh alongside Archer and Bell, Noel walks several paces ahead of his band mates. His demeanour can be read as either grumpy or thoughtful, but the contrast between him and the other members, not to mention the self-imposed isolation, gave a hint of the way the band's dynamic was proceeding and was almost a cartoon image of how the split would run. In interviews on the documentary, Noel's regular jokes are greeted with laughter from his band mates as usual. But was it reading too much in to say the laughter seems more reserved? This was a band, despite their growing musical maturity, who seemed ill at ease and the growing confidence of Bell and Archer within the setup seemed to sit uncomfortably with Gallagher. Now their position within the band contrasted noticeably with their unable-to-believe their luck attitude when they first joined.

Elsewhere, Gallagher's collaborations with his musical heroes continued. The influence of the Stone Roses on Gallagher's music had been hard to overstate. Since becoming famous, he had become friends with lead singer, Ian Brown. In 2004, Gallagher had given Brown the structure of a song he'd contributed to the *X Files* movie soundtrack, 'Teotihuacan' – named after the remains of the city north of Mexico City abandoned for suitably *X File* mysterious reasons which Gallagher had visited during an Oasis tour. With Gallagher's guitar it became 'Keep What Ya Got', the first single on Brown's solar effort *Solarized*. It hit UK No 18 after Brown had reworked it. 'It took me about four days to de-Oasis it and make it sound like a combination of the two of us,' said Brown.

Brown might have 'de-Oasised' Gallagher's track but, with the help of his band mates, Gallagher had 're-

Oasised' Oasis. *Don't Believe The Truth* had, in the eyes of many, been the band's best album since ...*Morning Glory*. However, a hovering cloud never seemed to be far away from Gallagher's thoughts. As the critics spoke glowingly of that most 21st century of occurrences in music – the 'return to form', Gallagher was reassessing his priorities. After all, he had parenthood to contend with, an experience he was finding to be a mixed bag. Within one interview he variously described being a father as 'a big responsibility,' 'one of life's greatest things,' and a 'pain in the arse.'

After Liam got in a fight in Munich, reportedly losing his teeth two front teeth, his elder brother spoke of them both being too old to behave in such ways. This became a running theme for him in both interviews and song. 'I used to be a geezer, a lad,' he told the *NME*. 'Now I'm a .... "man"?' On 'Just Getting Older' – the b-side to the single release of *The Hindu Times* – he took a sideways look at how life evolved over time and the way that the old pursuits don't have quite the same allure when you've got a few years behind you. In 2003, he said: 'I see myself having another five years in the band and then I'll do something else. I think it's sad when you're 40 and you're still pretending to be a gang. I won't be doing this when I'm 41.' His words would prove to be prophetic almost to the point of precision. There was more to come from Oasis, but Gallagher was finding himself increasingly uncomfortable. To mix football and tribal metaphors, The

Chief was losing the dressing room. For the remainder of the band's existence Noel would increasingly become the member who dwelt alone.

OUT OF TIME

'I THOUGHT THAT LOVE WOULD LAST
FOR EVER: I WAS WRONG.'
WH AUDEN, 'STOP ALL THE CLOCKS' (1936)

The Glastonbury 2008 line-up was announced in spring and while Oasis weren't down for the festival, the choice of rapper Jay-Z to headline led to many raised eyebrows. Inevitably, Gallagher's were more conspicuous than most. For all the festival's reputation for being cutting edge, the main slots were always supposed to be a reliably good time and that had always meant guitar bands. When Noel Gallagher expressed his surprise at the move, he once again found himself in the middle of media controversy. For much of the early part of the year he would have to be explaining what he meant in the face of all the inferences the press were drawing.

'The way it's played itself out is that I said Jay-Z had no

right to play Glastonbury, which is a crock of horseshit,' he told *Spin*. 'I got off a plane and someone asked me about the fact that Glastonbury hadn't sold out for the first time in years, and if it was because of Jay-Z. I innocently mused that that was probably right.' At this point in the game, both of them had more in common than they did differences in being stars at the top of their profession. 'I've seen his show. It's not my bag, but it's all right. We have a mutual friend in Chris Martin. So I am a guy who doesn't like hip-hop – shock, horror.' Even here he was doing himself down, having been intrigued by the 1980s pioneers as hip hop began to get big.

But if nothing else, the incident showed how, on a slow news day, every last pronouncement by Noel Gallagher could still make headlines, even so many years into his career. He didn't once again list the diverse music that had inspired him when he was starting out, but it seemed the media had him too firmly wedged in his traditionalist pigeonhole to listen even if he had. As unimportant as the Jay-Z argument was, the comments seemed to cause more of a storm than the eventual break-up of Oasis itself, just over a year later.

There had been hints of it as early as 2006, when a best-of called *Stop the Clocks* was issued in November, but Gallagher moved quickly to dispel suggestions that this marked a full stop on the band's career. This was just an extra album for fans to look forward to following the end of the Don't Believe the Truth tour. He explained the prosaic reason for the collection was contractual – the Oasis deal with Sony was about to come to an end and the company might have been able to issue a best of without input from anyone in the band. But Oasis were by then in a position where such opaque discussions had very real little impact on what they wanted to do. They would eventually sign to Sony BMG in a deal which allowed their Big Brother label much more input into how they were sold. Underlining how the band had no plans to split up, the eventual deal would be for three more albums.

The more immediate practical upshot was that Gallagher oversaw the selection and production of the album and, despite any reluctance he might have felt about such a release at this point in the Oasis story, it became something of an epic. *Stop the Clocks* would be a 18-track double album, ranging over a best of everything, the studio albums, the singles and the b-sides. Yet the title track, already held off from *Don't Believe the Truth*, would not see the light of day while Oasis were together and while there was little from their post-1997 output, there was nothing from *Be Here Now*. Gallagher was typically pragmatic about the listing. 'Yeah, of course. We're talking about the best of Oasis here,' he said to the *Guardian*. 'If you stop the man in the street and ask, "What's Oasis's best album?" a few might say *Don't Believe the Truth*, which is great, but the squares will say ...*Morning Glory* and the cool people will say *Definitely Maybe*. That album should just be called the *Best of Oasis*. Look. I was a superhero in the '90s. I said so at the time. McCartney, Weller, Townsend, Richards... my first album's better than all their first albums. Even they'd admit that.'

It was as contradictory as anything involving Gallagher and Oasis. On one hand it was extravagant, a double album that leaned heavily towards their early work. And yet it demanded to be heard on its own terms, with no new songs on it to give fans another reason to buy it. Even so, *Stop the Clocks* was a strong collection that would eventually sell over 2.5 million copies worldwide, though it didn't quite make the top spot in the UK charts, rather unfortunately being kept off by boyband Westlife and *The Love Album*.

For *NME* it was a full 10 out of 10, 'a faultless record compiled by a band riddled with faults.' There was no equivocation. 'To understand these songs is to know what it feels like to be 18 years old, with a great haircut and a great set of clothes, walking into a club with more heart and hope than dough, and thinking – metaphorically, at least – "Everyone in this shithole is going to suck my fucking dick."'

Drowned in Sound thought it significant that Gallagher himself had overseen the track listing. Although he had said that it was the length of the tracks on *Be Here Now* counted against them, they noted that little from the following albums made it on either. Nevertheless, they concluded, 'Despite a good decade or more having passed since the majority of these songs were recorded, Oasis's heyday really does feel like yesterday. Like it's been 24 hours since the last time you burst into song about being a rock'n'roll star or that you were sniffing Alka Seltzer through a cane.'

Gallagher seemed to have wholeheartedly embraced the idea of the best of. A documentary from the Don't Believe the Truth tour was given a limited cinema release to accompany the album and it shared its title with a new song that had been held off the previous studio recording sessions, *Lord Don't Slow Me Down*. The film was soon shown on Channel 4 while Gallagher and Gem Archer set off on a mini-world tour to promote the package with showings of the documentary and largely acoustic gigs late in 2006 and into the new year, including dates in Canada, UK, USA, Australia, Tokyo and Russia. Gallagher seemed to be at his most relaxed and expansive during these dates. It was the best of both worlds, at once a solo outing, but not a tour given too much publicity and not marketed as such. He could be fronting it without having to put on the performance that a full Oasis gig implied. Underlining his musical bond with Archer and armed only with guitars and keyboard, the duo performed tracks ranging from 'The Importance of Being Idle' to 'Talk Tonight' with drums from Terry Kirkbride of Proud Mary, the band which had been the first to be signed to Gallagher's Sour Mash label. The intimate size of the venues meant that Gallagher was able to banter with audiences but without the expectation of a big show was able to sit and concentrate on his work. In March 2007 the trio performed one of Gallagher's periodic charity shows at the Albert Hall for the Teenage Cancer Trust which, augmented by Paul Weller, was issued as *The Dreams We Have as Children*. After leaving Oasis it would be with the same trio plus keyboardist Jay Darlington and London choir the Crouch End Festival Chorus that Gallagher made his first live appearance in 2010.

With the success of *Don't Believe the Truth* infusing media reports on Oasis with adjectives such as 'revitalised', Gallagher seemed to be feeling much bolder. 'For the next record I really fancy doing a record where we just completely throw the kitchen sink at it,' he said. 'We haven't done that since *Be Here Now*.' He was talking of a full orchestra and maybe a choir. 'I think since *Standing on the Shoulder of Giants* we've been trying to prove a point of just bass, drums, guitar and vocals and nothing fancy. But I kind of like fancy!'

Recording began towards the end of summer 2007 on what would be *Dig Out Your Soul*, the title a play on DJs playing good soul music and the process of finding yourself, and would continue after Christmas when work shifted to Los Angeles. Producer Dave Sardy returned from *Don't Believe the Truth* to produce again and was refreshingly unsentimental about kicking off in Abbey Road. The band had returned for the first time since *Be Here Now* and he put some of the myths to rest. 'So much has changed in a place like Abbey Road,' said Sardy. 'It's not the studio it was back in the '60s, for so many reasons. We had them wheel in a mint-condition EMI TG console [1960s' mixing desk], and we placed it in the original position where it used to sit. And Noel and I brought in a bunch of our own gear, so we had two Neve Melbourne sidecars [vintage mixers] along with the TG console. They sounded great. Noel looked at me and said, "Ah! Now I know the secret to Abbey Road: you have to bring in a million dollars of your own gear!"'

For the most part, it was Gallagher himself on guitar while Archer played bass, Bell was on keyboards and Zak Starkey drummed. Producer Dave Sardy had asked if any in the band had songs with grooves, which would be the defining sound of the record, and everyone contributed. There was an almost equal writing split this time around – six songs were by Gallagher and five by the others (three from Liam and one each from the other two permanent members). For Gallagher, there was something particularly productive in his work with Sardy which seemed reminiscent of those very early sessions with Owen Morris, though he was never specific about what worked so well. 'No. Never,' said Sardy. 'I assume it's because we do good work together. And I think there's probably a lot of similarities between Manchester and Brooklyn. We're the same people. Our histories are the same, we're the same age, we both come from families without a tradition of music, and we both come from working class backgrounds where nobody was giving us a leg up. So we speak the same language. We have a mutual respect that we don't really talk about because we're busy working all day.'

The brothers themselves didn't write together. Perhaps

this in itself would be part of the process that would prepare them for working apart, but for now Noel himself said that he preferred writing on his own. Collaborating hadn't always been easy for him and after so long working up all the songs himself he had simply never considered writing with his brother. 'We all write separately and none of us kinda discuss what we're writing, because that would be ridiculous,' he said. Yet there was a remarkably cohesive feel to the latest output. Partly it was a feel, the preference over groove over the merits of particular songs on the new album which came with Sardy's input, but otherwise it seemed from what Gallagher said about work in the studio to be coincidental. There a number of songs which addressed God in their lyrics but this had no more significance than usual given the separate contributions. 'Without discussing the lyrical content they all seem to tie in, really,' said Gallagher. 'If there was a concept it wasn't fucking put there by me.'

Despite the positive talk going into the album, the shifting relationship between the brothers proved as resistant to analysis as ever. The rest of the band had recorded the instrumental tracks in Abbey Road while Liam had not laid down any vocals and that left just the two-week mixing period early in 2008 in Los Angeles in which to do it. But when Liam left the USA to get married on Valentine's Day to former All Saints' star Nicole Appleton, he was said not to have let the rest of the band or Noel know beforehand. In the pressurised time frame that meant two tracks were never completed. One song later appeared on ...*High Flying Birds* as '(I Wanna Live in a Dream) In My Record Machine'. In its final version it was an ambitious arrangement, its instrumentation featuring the symphonic choir which had been intended for the 2008 release before work switched to LA.

The brothers would characteristically differ as to the reasons why the songs were left off. On the one hand there was Liam, having his wedding in the middle of their working period, while on the other there were those incomplete songs, which weren't amended at any point before the album's release date – much later that year. As Noel later said, 'With us, what happens, happens. That's the album we came home with.'

Instead of the two epics, tracks intended as b-sides – '(Get Off Your) High Horse Lady' and Liam's 'Ain't Got Nothing' were used instead, giving the album a different feel. Gallagher and Archer also used the extra time to demo what became 'Dream On' on ...*High Flying Birds*. 'It's a bit throwaway,' said Gallagher later, 'but it's a got a great "She's Electric", "Digsy's Dinner"-esque quality to it.'

The rest of the album proceeded more smoothly and that was reflected in its overall sound. 'Bag it Up' was a strong opener, an energetic statement of intent. 'Ain't Got Nothin'' was Liam's account of the fight he was involved with in Germany back in 2002. Coming on like the Door's 'Five to One', 'Waiting for the Rapture' said Gallagher, 'is a story about meeting somebody in Ibiza in 2000 in Space.' This was the first time he had met Sara MacDonald. 'When I met them I was like, "Fucking hell." It was the person I've spent the last eight years with and it was kind of... I guess it's a very poetic way of saying, 'Will you go out with me?'" Like much of the album, this was a muscular blast, full of character and atmosphere. This was a band which had never sounded better.

Yet *Dig Out Your Soul* concluded with the mournful coda of the aptly titled 'Soldier On'. It was wrapped in the rich production which characterised the album but a downbeat ending to the last release of all, its echo sounding further than 14 years away from the roar which announced *Definitely Maybe* with 'Rock'n'Roll Star'.

Oasis was still, at heart, all about the relationship between the two brothers. But while it had once been a source of fascination and had powered the band's music, it was now increasingly opaque and introverted. It didn't really matter who was in the right about the rumbling arguments over songs and sessions. Seven studio albums in and they were still orbiting around the same dynamic. Noel had realised his earliest dreams against all predictions and all the odds. He'd heard all those who had said it was the end of the line for Oasis after *Be Here Now*. He had seen Oasis come back with a new line-up and now they were praised all over again with their most recent releases. But he had a family, was approaching his 40s and it was difficult for anyone watching from outside to see what else might make the difference in that underlying family dynamic.

For his own part, Gallagher wasn't sure that he should still be making music at an age when he would have been dismissed by his younger self. But he knew there was nothing else that he wanted to do and even when an interviewer asked him what would happen if Oasis came to a close, the answer had nothing of *Logan's Run* about it. 'I would eventually get back on stage doing it because that's what I do but... I mean, I still always look at Neil Young and Weller and think, "Well, as long as they're still going it's all right'. Once Weller retires then I've got ten years left on him, because he's ten years older than me, so he legitimises what I do.'

Zak Starkey had played on much of the album but in May it was announced that he was leaving the band. Chris Sharrock was the replacement, Gallagher suggesting the appointment had come in the face of objections from the younger half of the brotherly double act. 'Liam thought we should have got some 16-year-old in. I was like, "You're ludicrous! I'm fucking 40. I'm not playing in a band with some fucking kid who's gonna be marauding through the first class lounge, throwing heroin everywhere."' Although not a session drummer as such, Chris Sharrock had been around a number of bands on a long-term basis, from the Icicle Works via the Lightning Seeds to World Party. He'd even drummed on the La's 'There She Goes'. But the reason the new recruit annoyed Liam was, in his brother's words 'because he's Robbie Williams' drummer. I went home and I thought about it and it was just too much temptation to piss Robbie Williams and

Liam off in one phone call.' And so Sharrock was strapped in for the last year of the Oasis ride, arriving just in time to be invited along to Beady Eye. He made his live debut with the band for a filmed gig for fans in early August and the final tour started in North America towards the end of the month.

Even as the gigs got underway, Gallagher was again mooting the idea that something solo was in the offing. At the time though, there was still no suggestion that it would be a more permanent arrangement. 'I'd like for us to do separate projects after this new album. We'd all have to agree on it, so it will probably never happen. I've got loads of new songs. Somewhat predictably, they're all brilliant.'

But even before the internal problems in the band began to move that process to its abrupt conclusion, shows had to be cancelled after Gallagher was injured on stage less than two weeks into the tour. Someone had come out of nowhere at the V Festival in Toronto on 7 September and shoved him. Gallagher landed heavily on his monitors and cracked some ribs. Oasis didn't resume live duties until October as the album came out, preceded at the end of September by 'The Shock of the Lightning'.

NME welcomed the record. 'There's a new-band urgency and invention to it, a sense that Oasis are no longer straining to "be Oasis".' Their summary of the opening track might have stood for the album as a whole – 'It's still unmistakably Oasis, but it's playful, less obvious and unafraid of going into unexpected places.' Drowned In Sound agreed that the band were no longer so tied to their legacy. And this was a good thing. 'On a number of levels, this isn't so much Oasis hitting their stride as trying to sidestep expectation. When they remove themselves from their comfort zone, they are frequently interesting and occasionally superb.'

The band got back to the live routine and Gallagher at last got to play with the Crouch End Festival Chorus. He had first heard the choir playing the film music of Ennio Morricone in 2003 and had been interested for some time in doing something with them. While they hadn't made it onto *Dig Out Your Soul*, they backed Oasis at the BBC's Electric Proms at the Roundhouse in London for six songs though, as *Uncut* observed, the 50-strong choir 'were barely audible over the loudness of Oasis'. It was only as 'I Am the Walrus' provided the customary closer that the choir were able to make an impact. Gallagher would enjoy a long association with the Chorus and they formed something of a bridge between Oasis and his solo work. Not only were they augmenting the band at this very late stage but they would be part of his first live foray after the split at the Albert Hall in 2010 and went on to accompany the High Flying Birds on some of their high profile dates in the summer of 2012. When the solo album went over 600,000 sales in 2012, Gallagher had the platinum disc inscribed to choir conductor David Temple and sent to him as a thank-you.

For now Oasis continued with a reminder of their own past accompanying *Dig Out Your Soul*'s second single in

December. 'I'm Outta Time' featured a remix by Twiggy Ramierz, bassist and guitarist with Marilyn Manson. He and Gallagher had become good friends and Marilyn Manson himself was – improbably enough when it came to the alt.rocker's alt.rocker – a fan of Oasis, according to Gallagher. '*Be Here Now* is his favourite album,' claimed Gallagher, 'because it was recorded on a fucking mountain of charlie.'

In February Gallagher received an unexpected accolade in the shape of an award for Best Band Blogger in the *NME* annual ceremony. It underlined what was a natural facility for communicating as he hadn't come to the medium through any great love of gadgets. While many users of blogs and Twitter work hard to create exactly the right tone for their brand and yet fail to write anything of interest at all, Gallagher hadn't even got a computer when he started the blog. He would just send in his diary musings to be published by the Oasis site, but his natural knack for a good story was particularly suited to the informality of blogging. His thoughts on the attack the previous September were singled out for particular praise and for someone who had often said that there was no career for him outside of music, he was proving to be an accomplished writer in different areas. But his primary business was still doing well – *Dig Out Your Soul* had already sold more than 1.5 million copies worldwide and Oasis won the *NME* overall award for best British band, beating competition from young upstarts in the shape of Alex Turner's supergroup the Last Shadow

Puppets as well as youngish upstarts Muse and favourite old time foes Radiohead.

It was a promising start to the year for a revitalised Oasis, but the new chapter it seemed to be opening for Noel Gallagher had taken its dramatically different direction by the end of the summer. Within a year of the split followed the greatest hits compilation that, unlike *Stop the Clocks*, Gallagher had long said would only be released when Oasis were done. Taking the form of all 27 singles with bonus material, the package featured no new songs, as with the more personal survey Gallagher had assembled in *Stop the Clocks* just four years and one studio album earlier. Yet this last entry served as an unanswerable statement of their impact on the charts. They had now three compilations, with *The Masterplan* having collected some of Gallagher's most subtle b-sides back in 1999, but of all of them this was a much more straightforward parting of the ways. It was a substantial offering in size but a strikingly linear telling of the story. Even the title *Time Flies... 1994–2009* was perfunctory, the guest at a party who has just realised they've got something more interesting to be doing and disappears with a muttered platitude.

But that farewell seemed to have something of Noel Gallagher's own character about it, for all the sentiment of a Mancunian who doted on his mother and his Man City, always good at moving on. From Manchester itself, much later from a lifestyle that didn't suit him even though rock'n'roll was seductive enough to have claimed many other victims. Now he briskly disentangled himself from the band that had been his life for almost two decades and the relationship with his brother that defined it and took time out what to think to do next. Gallagher wouldn't thank anyone for comparing him to Damon Albarn, but the Blur frontman was always able to see what it was he needed to do to move on and to do it.

Acknowledging their biggest moment, the *Time Flies...* artwork was a view from the stage, no band member visible, of the Knebworth 1996 crowd, the cloudy blue sky taking up more than half the frame as the sea of people stretched out eternally towards the horizon. And if there was a guiding concept to the sequencing, Gallagher said it was to mimic the set list of a gig – 'albeit a fucking long one' – made up of a last blast of the hits.

But even making *Time Flies...* the ultimate night out with Oasis could not be a full stop on the band. Interest wouldn't disappear when there was still the long-running soap opera between the two brothers for commentators to cover. In the years after Noel's departure, they would often talk to each other through the press, sometimes through lawyers and they would follow each other's progress. Every so often talk of a reunion would be mooted, by an interviewer if not by one of the brothers themselves. And despite the very genuine arguments the two had with each other, nothing had happened which ruled that out entirely. Oasis had always been good at marking anniversaries and Noel Gallagher had shown he had no difficulty embracing his past as much as that of any other band. With so many other 1990s acts reforming, from the Stones Roses and Happy Mondays to Pulp and Blur, it would be a very confident punter who would bet against sometime around August 2014 being marked with 20 years of *Definitely Maybe*.

Noel Gallagher had after all spent many years building up to his first solo release in 2011 and he had been in no hurry to make the move. It was just that with each successive Oasis release he showed how he not only had the talent to write the songs, but he could develop and was willing to put the time in to work out how to become that authoritative figure leading his own band rather than directing operations from the side. *Noel Gallagher's High Flying Birds* had show-cased some of his strongest and most appealing songs and left him open to do anything he wanted. He had already laid claim to his Oasis heritage in his live set. If he wanted to, he could continue with his solo work as there was an enthusiastic appetite for his live appearances among festival crowds who would have hardly been born when he first had a UK No 1. He had even made good on Oasis's cancelled performance at Rock En Seine in France in 2009 when the High Flying Birds played the festival three years later with the Black Keys headlining.

Having made such an elegant transition between Oasis and his solo life there was no reason why he couldn't shuttle back again. He would certainly not be in the position of being forced into it for the money and more than anything it was, he said in 2011, almost as if the songs themselves demanded it. 'I think it's a shame that songs like "Champagne Supernova", "Rock'n'Roll Star", "The Importance of Being Idle" and "The Shock of the Lightning" will never be played again. In a stadium. That kind of fills me with sadness.' There would be plenty enough Oasis fans to fill that stadium and he had said himself that he would never able to or want to play to that size of crowd on his own. He would need Liam and Oasis with him, no matter how much he wanted to work in his own time and on his own terms. There was no material reason for him to go through the process of getting the old band back together again. But if anyone might try to sweep all before them just one more time, just for the hell of it, that would be Noel Gallagher.

DISCOGRAPHY

This is not intended as an exhaustive list of all Oasis and solo releases by Noel Gallagher. What follows are the major releases and UK and US chart placings to give an idea of the scope of the work and some of the more interesting b-sides.

OASIS

ALBUMS

	UK	US
Definitely Maybe (Creation 1994)	1	58
(What's the Story) Morning Glory? (Creation 1995)	1	4
Be Here Now (Creation 1997)	1	2
The Masterplan b-sides (Creation 1998)	2	51

Standing on the Shoulder of Giants (Big Brother 2000)	1	24
Familiar to Millions live (Big Brother 2000)	5	182
Heathen Chemistry (Big Brother 2002)	1	23
Don't Believe the Truth (Big Brother 2005)	1	12
Stop the Clocks best of (Big Brother 2006)	2	89
Dig Out Your Soul (Big Brother 2008)	1	5
Time Flies best of singles (Big Brother 2010	1	131

SINGLES

1994

'Supersonic'	31	11
('Take Me Away', 'I Will Believe')		
'Shakermaker'	11	–
('D'Yer Wanna Be a Spaceman?', 'Alive', 'Bring it on Down')		
'Live Forever'	10	2
('Up in the Sky', 'Cloudburst', 'Supersonic')		
'Cigarettes & Alcohol'	7	–
('I am the Walrus', 'Listen Up', 'Fade Away')		
'Whatever'	3	–
('(It's Good) to be Free', 'Half the World Away', 'Slide Away')		

1995

'Some Might Say'	1	28
('Talk Tonight', 'Acquiesce')		
'Roll With It'	2	24
('It's Better People', 'Rockin' Chair', 'Live Forever')		

'Wonderwall'   2   1
('Round Are Way', 'The Swamp Song', 'The
Masterplan')

1996
'Don't Look Back in Anger'   1   10
('Step Out', 'Underneath the Sky', 'Cum on Feel the Noize')

1997
'D'You Know What I Mean?'   1   4
('Stay Young', 'Angel Child', 'Heroes')
'Stand by Me'   2   5
('(I Got) the Fever', 'My Sister Lover', 'Going Nowhere')

1998
'All Around the World'   1   15
('The Fame', 'Flashbax', 'Street Fighting Man')

2000
'Go Let it Out'   1   14
('Let's All Make Believe', '(As Long as They've Got)
Cigarettes in Hell')
'Who Feels Love?'   4   –
('One Way Road', 'Helter Skelter')
'Sunday Morning Call'   4   –
('Carry Us All', 'Full On')

2002
'The Hindu Times'   1   –
('Just Getting Older', 'Idler's Dream')
'Stop Crying Your Heart Out'   2   –
('Thank You for the Good Times', 'Shout It Out Loud')
'Little By Little' / 'She is Love' double a-side   2   –
('My Generation')

2003
'Songbird'   3   –
('(You've Got) The Heart of a Star', 'Columbia')

2005
'Lyla'   1   19
('Eyeball Tickler', 'Won't Let You Down')
'The Importance of Being Idle'   1   –
('Pass Me Down the Wine', 'The Quiet Ones')
'Let There be Love'   2   –
('Sittin' Here in Silence (On My Own)', 'Rock'n'Roll
Star')

2007
'Lord Don't Slow Me Down'   10   –
(download only)

2008
'The Shock of the Lightning'   3   12
('Falling Down')
'I'm Outta Time'   12   –

2009
'Falling Down'   10   –
('Those Swollen Hand Blues')

SOLO

Noel Gallagher's High Flying Birds   1   5

SINGLES

2011
'The Death of You and Me'   15   –
('The Good Rebel')
'AKA...What a Life!'   20   48
('Let the Lord Shine a Light on Me')
'If I had a Gun'   95   25
('I'd Pick You Every Time')

2012
'Dream On'   52   –
('Shoot a Hole into the Sun')